The Next Right Step

From Teaching to EdTech

EVA BROWN

DEDICATION

To all teachers, who help children take the next step in learning every single day.

And to Jeff, for always being beside me as we take the next right step together.

CONTENTS

ACKNOWLEDGMENTS

Thank you to the many teachers who reached out to me to ask about EdTech. You sparked this idea.

Thank you to the current and former colleagues who so graciously gave of their time to provide feedback and support.

Thank you to my husband, Jeff, and to Shefali Parekh, for being such fantastic editors. Any mistakes still found in this book must have been added after you reviewed the text!

But mostly, thank you to my family. I could not have done this without your sacrifices as you gave up many Saturday mornings and weekday evenings with me as I worked on this project.
Thank you for believing in me.
I love you!

1

How Did You Get into EdTech, Anyway?

In February 2021, my InMail® notification chimed. "Hi Eva, I saw you were an Implementation Coordinator and would love to learn how you got started in your field and connect sometime." The writer was a teacher, someone I had never met before, who just happened to come across a post that I had shared about my new position. She continued, "As a current teacher, what skills would you say would make me a successful candidate to get hired for a company like [yours] if you don't mind me asking?" Recently I had been asked the same question by some friends who were still in the classroom, so I set up an online session to answer their questions live.

The session was so lively and rich with questions that I decided to offer another one. I enjoy speaking with people and sharing my story, and the teachers were eager for knowledge. After having to pivot so many times during the past year, from creating take-home assignments to teaching virtually to returning to the classroom with masks, they seemed even more interested in answering the question of how else they might be able to use their skills and experience to impact students and education. I arranged for another session, limiting the capacity to 10 people to allow for conversation. I posted an open invitation, and within minutes, that session was full.

From there, the idea of this book was born. As questions continued to pour into my inbox from people I had never met before, I realized how hungry teachers were to learn how to take the next step into the business world when all their experience was in a classroom. The questions were always the same. How did I make the leap? What positions should they consider? How should they prepare for different positions? What are the salaries like? What are the pros and cons? There was often a tone of discouragement, with teachers sharing that they had been looking for months with no luck. There were so many requests to connect that I couldn't possibly keep up with them all, but I read all the messages and mapped out the contents of this book so that I could share some answers not only with those who had already reached out but also those who were starting to wonder about possibilities beyond the classroom.

The thing is, I never planned to leave the classroom. From as far back as I can remember, my favorite game to play was "school." During the warm, upstate New York summers, when the neighbors were available and willing, we would set up a classroom of sorts on one of our front porches. Whoever had prepared the most worksheets got to be the teacher, and it was almost always me. Initially we would copy each worksheet several times by hand, until I discovered carbon copy paper, which was a game-changer. I would make math sheets, reading passages, and science activities asking my "students" to determine which leaf matched which tree. I established classroom rules (1. Be on time; 2. Raise your hand to talk; 3. Don't rub burdock in anyone's hair). And I planned field trips to my favorite tree in the woods or gathering the smoothest rocks from the creek by their house to categorize as sedimentary, igneous, or metamorphic.

As summer turned to cool fall and everyone went back to "real" school, I turned my teaching attention to my Fisher-Price people, setting up the plastic one-room schoolhouse on my floor and arranging the plastic desk chairs into different configurations to see how I could best meet the needs of all my one-inch-tall students. I would beg my father, an actual science teacher, to let me grade his students' tests until the advent of Scantron (which I secretly hated since it removed the necessity for my help.) I begged my own teachers to let me teach whenever I could, working out ways to explain two-digit by two-digit multiplication or the best strategies for learning to read.

I was born to teach.

As a college student, I majored in elementary education because my other interests were so varied that I couldn't choose just one subject to focus on as a secondary education teacher. I didn't want to teach *just* English or history or math—I wanted to teach *all* the subjects. I did my internships in primary classes in both the United States and England and loved every minute of it. I read every book I could find and watched every movie that was released that focused on teachers who changed students' lives. My heroes were principal Joe Louis Clark, Laura Ingalls Wilder (for teaching so many different students in one classroom), Anne Sullivan, and Howard Gardner (who so perfectly captured what teachers already know – that *every* student is gifted in some way, and that school only measures *some* areas of gifting and intelligence.) And of course, the teacher who had changed my life – Mr. Ed Sharpe, my 8th grade health teacher, who helped me step out of anxiety and the fear of being bullied and step into a world of possibility, teaching me something that would never be measured on any state test.

As I transitioned from the college classroom to my own

classroom, I worked with 28 squirmy second graders in a new charter school outside of Boston. It was there that I was introduced to Harry Wong's *The First Days of School*, which probably saved me from quitting after the first year since college was filled with classes on educational theories and few on classroom management. Those first three years were challenging but reinforced the idea that I was born to teach. I loved teaching!

In 2000, I moved to Virginia and began teaching fourth grade. It was during my years there that No Child Left Behind became law, and although standardized testing had been a part of education for over three decades by that time, there was a new focus on making sure *every* student passed a state test. It was the same test for all my students, including Logan (name changed), who had been neglected and abused for his first nine years of life, witnessed the death of his sister at the hands of his abuser, and couldn't write anything other than his own name. It was there that I learned that good intentions of political movements like No Child Left Behind do not always appreciate the true nature of the classroom. My goal for Logan that year was not to get him to pass a fourth-grade reading test; it was to help him heal and learn to trust so he wouldn't flinch every time I walked by him, and to start him on his educational path by introducing him to letters and letter sounds. At the end of that year, he didn't pass the test. But he did spontaneously hug me on his last day and declare, "I love you, Miss Wilson."

I was born for that moment.

My years in the classroom continued as I taught fifth grade and then, after completing a master's degree in teaching reading and moving to Florida, intensive reading to students just like Logan: 12–17-year-old students who couldn't yet read. Some had severe learning disabilities, some had been incarcerated, some had been in and out of school as they moved with their migrant parents, and almost all were from incredibly poor families. I was a teacher who knew my students were highly unlikely to score "proficient" on the state reading test at the end of the year. They were starting at a kindergarten or first grade level and, therefore, it was near impossible for most of them to make 6–8 years of growth in one year. They were the "bottom quartile," and my job, according to the state, was to "show learning gains." Which they did. According to the state, I was a "highly effective teacher."

Well, thank you for that.

In 2006, I was given the opportunity that changed the course of my future in education. I became a literacy/instructional coach in my county, working with middle school teachers across all content areas. In this role, I met Carol, an educational leader in my district. Working closely with her, I studied and read more educational research and books than I had since pursuing my masters, learning new reading theories, adult learning practices, and methods like backwards planning. I had the opportunity to visit dozens of classrooms, supporting teachers throughout my home school and district, and I designed professional development to help them learn the strategies that Carol was teaching me.

Carol left the district after another year or two when she was given an incredible opportunity to become the director of training for a large educational publishing company. But we kept in touch, and in 2010, she reached out to me to ask if I might be interested in doing some part time training for the company in schools and districts throughout the state around a specific reading intervention. We met for lunch, and she shared the program I would be training on to help teachers begin their implementation. It excited me to see a program so richly capture every aspect of reading theory that she and I had studied together. I said yes.

That was the start of my transition from the classroom to what is now called the "EdTech" world. I was given an unexpected and unsought opportunity, and I took it. I never planned to leave the classroom full time. I thought I would train once a month or so as needed. I kept working as a literacy coach in the district and served as a "regional consultant" doing part time work when I could for this company.

That one opportunity changed the course of my career. In 2011, I made the transition fully out of the classroom. My reasons were multifold. The main reason was that I thought, incorrectly, that my husband and I would be leaving Florida in the near future. I wanted to keep the job that would allow me to go anywhere in the world, so I resigned from my position at the school district and began to accept more assignments from Carol. But there were also other reasons, initially. The pay was much better for the regional consulting work than for working in the district. And it also didn't involve (at least initially) giving up every weekend to plan for lessons the next week. It seemed, on the surface, like I would have more time available for my family and less stress.

I was still teaching, but now I was teaching teachers.

Since that time, I have worked in numerous roles at two large educational publishing companies and a small EdTech start-up. I have been a trainer, a consultant, a coach, an implementation coordinator, a client success manager, and a project manager for several different projects in both small and large districts, working with schools around the nation and training teachers all over the world. I have experienced the pros and cons of working for a large corporation and a small company. I have also had the privilege of partnering with hundreds of teachers, principals, and superintendents around the nation as a coach and consultant and have witnessed firsthand the stresses educators continue to be under. At least a quarter of the individuals I work with in schools ask me how I got into this field and how they might be able to get into it. The teachers who ask the most are those who have been teaching for 4-8 years or those close to retirement looking for some work to do on the side. They all talk about the stress of the classroom and how they just don't see how they can continue in the field of education much longer.

Covid-19 made this much more acute. The stress of teaching during the 2020–2021 school year led many teachers to seek new roles outside of education. Education shifted literally overnight – for most in America, on one day in March 2020, school buildings shut down and teachers were told to transition to online learning. Some had to create lessons overnight. Some had a "generous" week or two to create a plan. But all of them faced uncertainty and fear with their teaching like they never had before, with reports of teachers breaking down in tears on Zoom® sessions with their students when they couldn't figure out how to help a student turn on their microphone or find their assignment in their learning management system. Parents could now sit in on students' classes and critique teachers, who were doing what I call "crisis teaching." There was little to no research prior to 2020 on the most effective ways to teach online, synchronously or asynchronously, and teachers were tasked with being "highly effective" as virtual teachers with no clear idea of how to do so.

It's no surprise then that many of them felt like teaching was no longer something they could do. Even if they had previously thought they were born to teach, it no longer felt possible. And the EdTech world began to look like a better option.

If that describes you, then this book is for you. If you, for this reason or some other, are trying to leave the classroom or school setting to make your way into the corporate world of education but have no idea how to do so, then I am glad you are reading.

Let me be clear. It is *not* my intent in this book to convince you to leave the classroom and move to the EdTech world. Rather, over the years as more and more teachers ask me to help them make this transition, I ask them to focus on what they are looking for. I try to help them understand not only what they *gain* by moving to the educational business world (whether that be publishing, EdTech, or consulting) but also what they would *lose*. There are definite pros to the work I now do. But there are also cons. And if you, like me, believe you were born to teach, knowing the balance of these pros and cons and weighing them for yourself is crucial.

Once we look at the pros and cons, I want to then share advice based on my experience of how you can make the transition to the corporate world if that is the direction you choose to go. Some of you, though, may put this book down after reading the pros and cons, deciding that maybe EdTech is not for you after all. And that, to me, is also a win. Because we need teachers to *stay* too. We need great teachers who love kids, who can keep their eyes focused beyond the state assessments and the politics and the low pay and the high stress. We need teachers to struggle through the school year, doing all they can in the classroom trenches, to raise up the next generation of teachers and leaders.

And we need teachers to remember that the 2020–2021 school year was a crisis year. As I spoke with teachers during this time, one teacher shared with me, "Teaching has been so stressful this year more than ever and it doesn't make me happy the way it used to." Another shared with me, "I love my kids (usually), but I live in a state where education is constantly under attack. This year has been worse than ever, and I am ready to see what else is out there."

2020–2021 will not be the norm. The level of stress felt during that year will not remain for every year. Yes, teaching is and always will be stressful, and teachers will often feel attacked by political endeavors, but the level of stress that teachers felt during 2020–2021 was higher, as it was for everyone in the world. Perhaps deciding to leave a field you were born to do should not happen based on a crisis snapshot in time.

On the other hand, burnout and frustration during a crisis are not the only reasons why teachers consider leaving the classroom. There are opportunities in the business world that one cannot necessarily have in a school. One teacher wrote, "I would like to remain a part of education, but would like to have a greater reach, and have more opportunity to grow outside of the school building." Another stated, "I have always been drawn to have an impact on education on a larger scale. I love growth and have a growth mindset. I started to feel like I wasn't growing career-wise teaching public school." And although some may argue that staying in a school setting and pursuing educational leadership would be a way to have "greater reach," the business world of education is another very valid way to do so.

There really is no one *right* way to move forward in your educational career. For some, staying in the classroom is the best option. For others, pursuing other roles within a school district, from coaching to administration, is the next best move. For still others, moving into a corporate (or even nonprofit) educational organization makes sense. So, for this reason, I would ask that before you continue reading, you ask some questions of yourself.

Consider the following reflection questions. Write down your answers, and maybe revisit them during a break when you aren't teacher-bone-weary from creating differentiated synchronous and asynchronous lessons for your students. Let your answers be your guide as you consider your next career move. And should you choose to stay right where you are, that is great. My goal is to help you take the next right step for *you* – and whether that is staying right where you are or moving into the corporate world, I have achieved that goal if you make an educated and confident career choice.

****

REFLECTION QUESTIONS

1. Why did you go into teaching to begin with? What did you dream teaching would be like?
2. What are you afraid you will miss if you leave the classroom?
3. What are you excited to leave behind if you leave the classroom?
4. What are you looking for in a new role? What do you see yourself doing that would excite and renew you? What do you want to be doing?
5. What do you want your "off-work" time to look like?
6. What do you *imagine* a job in the EdTech or other educational business world is like?
7. What are your must-haves in a job?
8. What are your definite things to avoid in a job (for example, extreme stress or being away from your family)?

2

What Are the Pros and Cons of Working in the World of Edtech?

Over the course of the past year, I have communicated with hundreds of teachers who have shared their reasons for desiring to move into the EdTech industry. When I have asked why they desire to move, almost all the teachers mentioned low pay and the level of unprecedented stress in the classroom.

The inability to retain good teachers is not a new problem. The media focused on the stress levels of teachers especially during the 2020–2021 school year, when teachers around the world faced the challenge of virtual or blended learning for the first time coupled with new restrictions on social interaction in the classroom. However, even prior to 2020, retention rates of teachers had been an ongoing concern. According to the 2020 PDK poll (which, it is important to note, was written in 2020 but based on questions asked in 2019, prior to Covid's effects on schools):

- 60% of teachers responded that they were unfairly paid. That varied widely by region, with 60% of teachers in the Northeast reporting that they believed their pay was fair versus only 28% of teachers reporting fair pay in the South.

- 75% of teachers reported that their schools were not receiving the funding needed.
- 50% of teachers reported that they had considered leaving the profession, with that rate being higher for high school teachers (61%) than for lower grade teachers (48%).
- Of the teachers who reported that they had considered leaving their profession, the top three reasons given were inadequate pay/benefits (22%), stress/pressure/burnout (19%), and lack of respect or feeling valued (10%).[1]

And this was *pre*-Covid-19!

This is not just an American problem. A report published by England's Department of Education in 2020 (using data from 2019) revealed that approximately 1 in 5 teachers left the field after their first year of teaching, with that number increasing to 1 in 3 teachers leaving within the first 5 years.[2]

The question is, what are the reasons teachers leave teaching at such high rates? And how does the turnover rate in teaching compare to the turnover rates in other careers? As teachers consider a career change, it is important for them to consider their reasons for wanting that change, as well as examine the information available to them about the job satisfaction and retention rates in other careers. It is impossible to fully understand the pros and cons of any career other than one's own, but examining them is important, as "the grass looking greener" on some other career path may actually just be an illusion.

A quick review of the research on job turnover reveals that education is not the only field with a retention problem. According to the U.S. Bureau of Labor Statistics, the annual "quits" (including those who left their job voluntarily for reasons other than retirement or transfers) in 2019 increased to their highest level ever in nine industries – with the highest increase ever recorded in the "top three" industries: accommodation and food services; professional and business services; and retail trade.[3]

Quitting a job may not be due to negative factors like high levels of stress, low pay, or unhappiness, of course. It may be that there was a life event that required a change or that someone quit one company to pursue a higher position or salary with another company. But when considering whether to leave a profession that one considered, at least at the start, a *calling*, it is important to weigh the reasons. If you are considering leaving teaching because you are burnt out, stressed or concerned about your pay, it would be wise to consider what these factors look like in the career you are looking to move into to make sure they really are a good fit. No career exists in utopia; there will be challenges in any position. What you need to consider is, what is the balance of pros to cons you are looking for, and what compromises are you willing to make?

So let's examine some of the top reasons teachers say they wish to pursue another career.

*****

PAY

A January 2020 (again, pre-Covid) article from CNBC reviewed data from the U.S. Bureau of Labor Statistics and found that in 2019, workers were leaving their jobs at the fastest rate ever recorded. The reason cited was pay. The author pointed out that in the current market, the best way for Americans to increase their salaries was to *leave* their current position and take a new one. This is because it is often easier to negotiate a higher starting salary than it is to negotiate a raise.[4] In the corporate world, there is no salary schedule in which all workers are given the same salary increase (although a cost-of-living adjustment each year is standard). In most cases, your salary is negotiated by you when hired – and a raise is not necessarily guaranteed. (Of course, this is also the case in teaching. But one key difference for teachers is that a union often fights for a contract for all teachers, with over 70% of teachers participating in unions as recently as 2017.[5] In the corporate world, this is not the case, with only about 2% of those in professional service careers participating in a union.)[6]

In 2019–2020, the national average salary of public school teachers in the United States was $63,645 according to the National Center for Education Statistics. Of course, that varies widely by state since education funding and salary schedules are not set at the federal level. This means that teachers in Mississippi are paid almost $20,000 less than that national average, at an average salary of $45,192, while teachers in New York earned an average of $87,543. In many states, the average salary has *decreased* significantly from a decade ago – likely due in part to the high rates of veteran teachers leaving the field and more novice teachers entering.[7]

These differing rates can be infuriating to teachers. However, it is important to note that even in the corporate world, the state in which you live will likely affect your pay. For example, at the time of this writing, ZipRecruiter.com reported a $25,000 difference in the average salary of customer success managers from the highest-paying state to the lowest. The highest-paying states for customer success managers were the same states that pay the highest teacher salaries – and the lowest states in education were the lowest for customer success. Cost of living in each region is a consideration in the salary offered.[8]

The fact that might surprise many teachers considering a move into EdTech is that this career change may *not* mean that you have higher pay. It will greatly depend on where you live, what you currently make as a salary, and what type of company you work for. For example, a customer success manager in Mississippi *may* make more on average than a classroom teacher, with the average salary for a customer success manager there reported at $50,971. However, teachers in New York *may* make significantly less than they would in the classroom, with an average customer success salary reported at $67,177.[9]

You also need to consider that no matter how many years of teaching you have had, a move into a new career path means that you are now back at entry level. You cannot expect that you will make the salary of a 10-year customer success manager even though you have had 10 years of experience as a classroom teacher. Moving to a new career means that you are starting, usually, at the bottom of the ladder or at least on a lower rung. If you are going to make this transition, keep that in mind. Your experience *does* matter – your insights into education are valuable for EdTech companies. However, you are a novice at your new career with a lot to learn. You might need to compromise on salary.

One final note to consider is that a teacher's salary is for 10 months of the year. Of course, many teachers spread this out over 12 months to make sure they have some money coming in during the summer months. Even more notably, many teachers do work during the summer planning for the upcoming school year on their own time, while others take on other work to generate more income. However, there is generally some flexibility with summers, with teachers being able to work around the needs of their families.

Teachers with children of their own may want to consider that any corporate job means you will not get summers off. You do not get two weeks off for the winter holidays or the same week off as your children for spring break. Any time you *do* take off comes out of your bank of personal days, and these can vary greatly from one company to another. Some companies have "flexible time off" – meaning they don't specify the number of days that you can take per year. (I don't know of *any* flexible time off companies, though, that would let me take off eight weeks in the summer to be with my children.) Other companies may give new hires 10–12 personal days per year and increase that over time.

And, although summers are generally the "recovery time" for teachers, for those in EdTech, summers are the busiest time of year. "Back-to-school" starts around the second or third week of July, as many students around the country return as early as the third week of July.[10] This means that the time of year your children have off tends to be the time of year that those in EdTech are the busiest. I worked for one company that denied any personal time off request from mid-July through November 1 for this reason. This time of year is "all hands on deck" for education companies. I actually know of one person who started her career in the corporate world and then switched to teaching so that she could have the summers with her children!

There is another side to this, though. One of the most difficult things for teachers during the school year is the stress of having to take a day off due to illness or personal leave. Writing lesson plans and entrusting students to a substitute teacher for even a day is difficult. I know many teachers who would rather work while sick than have to deal with the stress of writing sub plans. When working for a company, you do not have to create sub plans. Depending on your role, taking a day or two off for illness or an hour here or there for a doctor's appointment may be as easy as notifying your manager or team that you need the time off. (This is different for those who are consultants and trainers, though. These roles are often much more similar to teaching. If you have a full-day in-person professional learning session to facilitate, you may find that you work while sick. I did this numerous times. In one instance, I had to lead a seven-hour session for 50 people while suffering from a fever and laryngitis.) In general, though, taking time off for illness is usually easier, and that is a definite pro of EdTech work.

*****

STRESS

Each year, CareerCast.com reports on the year's most stressful positions and why. The 2019 report also contains some indicators as to why these positions are so stressful. Some of these careers are obviously stressful – with military personnel, firefighter, airline pilot, and police officer taking the top ranks. Some are more surprising, though. Taxi driver made the list. So did newspaper reporter and broadcaster. Teacher, amazingly, did not.[11]

CareerCast ranks job stress using 11 different indicators. These include:

- Job travel requirements
- Growth potential
- Deadlines
- Working in the public eye
- Competitiveness
- Physical demands
- Environmental conditions
- Hazards encountered
- Risk to one's own life
- Risk to the life of another person

- Meeting the public[12]

If we consider these 11 indicators, teaching has some definite stressors. Working in the public eye is one of the most common stressors I hear from teachers. There are just too many people "critiquing" teaching – from students and parents to politicians. Environmental conditions can be another stress factor, especially in lower-income or inner-city schools where facilities may be in disrepair or technology is not functioning properly. Environmental conditions are also impacted by student behavior and how much support or value a teacher experiences from the school leadership. And of course, there are other stressors that may fall into these categories depending on the teaching situation.

So, what are the stressors of working for an education company? What would be the stress trade-offs? These will vary from company to company. My encouragement to you is to consider these 11 factors – as well as the current stressor you really desire to leave behind – and use your own reflection to guide your search. What type of stress are you willing to have?

One top-11 stressor in the corporate world to consider is travel. Travel is often a part of careers in education-focused corporations. Consultants and customer success managers may be required to travel on-site to the schools and districts assigned to them. For some, this may be viewed as a perk of the job, especially if your company allows you to keep any airline and hotel points you accrue. (Not all companies do, though, so check. Don't assume.) But it is also important to consider the demands of travel on time and stress.

Business travel is not luxurious. You do not fly business or first class in most situations (unless you have accrued so many points that you can automatically upgrade). Your days are very long, and you are away from family and from pets.

Depending on the role, you may spend more time on the road than you do at home. For example, one company I worked for required full-time professional services consultants to be "on-site" with a customer at a school or district from Monday–Thursday, weekly. On-site was generally a long car ride or flight away, and often involved different sites in different states during the same week. On-site also generally meant being at the school for the full school day. To ensure that consultants were at a school on a Monday morning, many had to fly on a Sunday afternoon, rent a car and drive to a hotel (which might be several hours from the nearest airport), and prepare the night before. After the school day ended, they might have needed to drive back to the airport, return their car, and hop onto another flight to another school for the next day. It was not unusual for my colleagues to share stories of flight delays that caused them to arrive at their next destination after midnight, and then they still needed to rent a car, drive to their hotel, and be up at 6 a.m. so that they could be at the next school on time. They would do this several days a week, arriving home late at night on a Thursday (or even Friday morning). They had an "office day" on Friday, and then would start all over again on Sunday.

And during all this travel, consultants were required to write lengthy reports for each teacher they worked with and have those sent back to the teacher or administrator within 24–48 hours. They were also required to be constantly learning more about the company's new offerings and products so that they could be expert trainers and provide "soft upsells" (for although consultants are not usually also salespeople, they are expected to be constantly on the watch for ways the customer could benefit from additional products and services and mention this to the customer and sales representative).

Traveling consultants also had to think about their health. Eating nutritious meals is not easy when you are on the road so much. Although there is a "meal allowance", meaning that consultants generally have a certain amount they can spend for breakfast, lunch, and dinner, finding quality food when traveling takes time. Fast food can become a temptation as you dash from one site or airport to another. Other consultants might have food delivered to their hotel rooms while they are working on their reports at night. It isn't easy to take leftovers to schools the next day as hotel refrigerators are never cold enough to keep ice packs frozen. I know of a lot of consultants who would purchase a box of granola bars or container of nuts just to keep on hand in case they couldn't find anywhere to eat. And many of my colleagues (and I) purchased Fitbits out-of-pocket just to track their steps as they soon realized they were putting on weight.

Then there are the expense reports. Everything you spend while traveling needs to be accounted for. Receipts are due within a certain time frame. Every expense must be categorized and approved – and if it is not an approved expense, you will pay for it yourself. For example, I knew one person who purchased an ergonomic office chair for her home office but didn't get that approved ahead of time. She ended up covering that expense. Another person spent more than she was allotted at breakfast and ended up covering the difference. (In general, though, if you carefully read your expense policy, you can avoid this.) Expense reporting takes time to complete, and for those who travel, there are a *lot* of expenses!

Those who work part-time (or per diem) *may* have a little more flexibility in when and how often they travel. This will vary by company. It is important to know, though, that part time/per diem positions that pay by the hour and require travel often do not pay you the same rate for your travel time as for your work time. So, if you are considering a part-time position that requires travel, definitely ask about how or whether travel time is compensated during the final stages of the interview process.

Travel is by no means luxurious in the business world. It is exhausting and stressful – and I am someone who *loves* to travel in general. I once drove from Florida to Maine *for fun*, by myself. But the requirements of travel, and the stress on your time and on your family, is something to seriously consider and ask about. What are the travel expectations of any role you are considering, and what does the day in the life of someone in this role really look like?

Another stressor to consider in the corporate world of education would fall under the category of "deadlines." In teaching, there are definitely deadlines, especially with those 28 pairs of eyes looking at you daily. (I remember telling my friend years ago that it didn't really matter if she was late for work because she worked in an office. But if I were late for work, 28 seven-year-olds would be stranded on the playground. Not quite accurate, but I was trying to make a point.) Teachers have deadlines for teaching plans, grades, testing, committee work – and there is often a literal bell reminding them that time is up. As a teacher, I took work home with me almost every night, lugging students' writing journals and math books home in a rolling milk crate. I planned lessons and did even more grading every weekend. Teaching was most definitely not a job that was contained within an eight-hour work day.

What surprised me most, though, was that when I left teaching, this didn't change. In my various roles as a professional services consultant, trainer, coach, project manager, implementation coordinator, and client success manager, I also have not worked just a 40-hour week. Those on the road often work 12- to 15-hour days every day. As my work transitioned to more online work, I found that I was working more and more across time zones, and I often have meetings or calls outside of what would be considered my "normal" work hours. In my current position, colleagues work in a number of different countries, with at least one member living on the exact opposite side of the world than I do. Scheduling meetings with him requires flexibility.

Working remotely, there *is* more flexibility in my schedule than I would have in either an office, travel or classroom-based job. But I do not work *less* than I did as a teacher. I work *differently*.

Another area of stress for teachers is the evaluation process. Most American public school teachers are evaluated based on a variety of factors including a series of student and teaching "indicators" that are designed to show evidence of excellent teaching in combination with students' state test results. This system, though well intentioned, does not consider factors outside of a teachers' control – like whether or not the student comes from a supportive home, is being nourished on a regular basis, is frequently absent from school, moves from school to school throughout the year as parents migrate with jobs, or speaks English. Although teachers well know the value of differentiation, the different factors affecting the lives of their students are often not considered in their own professional evaluations.

It will be important for teachers considering a career change to ask the question, "How will I be evaluated in this new position?" As teachers, you are familiar with indicators on which you were measured. In corporations, there are also indicators of success, known as Key Performance Indicators (KPIs) and targets. These KPIs and targets are different ways to measure progress toward the overall goal. For example, a company's overall goal might be a certain amount of revenue. The KPIs often include customer retention rates, satisfaction rates, and amount of revenue brought in. The targets would be the percentage you aim to achieve, for example 90% of customers retained or 95% customer satisfaction ratings.

There are times when your KPIs will be affected by things outside of your control. For example, over almost a decade of leading training sessions for teachers, I came to expect at least one teacher in every session who would be disgruntled about the fact that their school had adopted the program I was training on. These disgruntled teachers often took their frustration out on the survey that went back to *my* supervisor. I learned to preface the survey by gently reminding teachers that the survey was about how I did as a trainer and *not* about how they felt about the school requiring them to use the program. However, it was still disheartening to see those surveys included into my satisfaction rating, even when the teacher would state that they thought I did a great job but that they didn't like the program or the fact that they were being required to use it.

In the EdTech world, your survey results will sometimes be affected by the fact that not all teachers are tech-savvy or have an understanding that software platforms are not changed by just a few keystrokes. I experienced this with one disgruntled customer who give me a 0% on the satisfaction rating after he asked me to change the way the platform worked. He was upset that the software was designed in a specific way, and he wanted it to work in a way it did not. I explained that I would share his input with the software development team and offered some work-arounds, however I (not being a coder) was unable to personally "fix" what he viewed as a problem with the platform. He wrote in that the service he received was terrible and that he would never recommend the product to others. That went on my internal report.

If your KPIs include customer retention or revenue growth, there will also be factors you cannot control. School funding changes on an annual basis. If you have a "bumper crop" one year because a district had a lot of funding, and then you lose that customer the next year when the funding goes away, that can impact your own company goals. This can be challenging for teachers to adjust to in the corporate world.

As I share about the stressors of moving into the corporate world of education, I am often asked what I miss the most about being in the classroom. That is easy to answer. There are two things I miss most about being a school-based educator: the students and my colleagues. There is nothing like seeing a student learn, being a witness to a student growing academically, emotionally, and personally. Nothing I have experienced in the corporate world can take the place of the 16-year-old student being able to read for the first time or the 10-year-old finally understanding how division works. Don't get me wrong – I love teaching adults too. But as a teacher, you know what I am talking about. That spark of learning in a classroom is irreplaceable.

But I also miss my colleagues. In every position I have held in the corporate world, I have been based from my home. That has been a blessing in many ways, but I do miss daily camaraderie with those working on the same mission I am. Remote work allows for many phone calls and video calls, but after Covid-19, we can all understand how that does not replace in-person collegiality. There are long hours or even days when I do not interact with my colleagues. When I was traveling a lot, weeks might go by when I didn't talk in some meaningful way with a colleague other than to send off a quick work-related email. And annual business retreats (when offered) cannot replace daily teamwork and interaction.

The lack of social interaction can really take a toll on those who thrive on this aspect of work. One of my colleagues recently left EdTech because she found the remote work depressing. She was not getting enough interaction, and it left her feeling empty as an extrovert. This certainly isn't the case for all extroverts in EdTech. However, if you transition into a role that will look similar, consider how you will fill your social needs with friends in your life.

*****

REFLECTION QUESTIONS

1. What do you dislike about your current job? What are you "running from"?
2. What is important to you and your family? What does your "day in the life" need to look like?
3. What is the lowest salary you are able and willing to accept? Are you ready to possibly have a *lower* salary than your current one?
4. Have you considered the impact of summer being the busiest time of year? How will that impact you and your family?
5. What is the "day in the life" of someone in the position that you are considering? What are their reported stressors? What do they miss about teaching, and what do they love or find challenging about their current position?
6. What are the goals and expectations (KPIs) of someone in the position you are considering?
7. After learning about these pros and cons, does the idea of this position still excite you? Is there a different position that might be a better fit, either in the corporate world *or* right where you are currently?

3

How Can I Experience Career Growth Right Where I Am?

The last chapter may have left you wondering if I am going to spend all my time trying to convince you not to leave the classroom. Not so! Although I do encourage you to examine whether this really is the right move for you, I also want to encourage you to seek the right opportunity for growth. If you have made the decision that a move out of classroom teaching is the right step for you, the question becomes, "What next?"

There are two main paths one could take out of the classroom and still be involved, in some way, in education. Both paths lead to opportunities that you may not have considered before, and both involve professional growth and challenges. In this chapter, we are going to explore different opportunities that exist for teachers on the first path – staying within a school district to advance your career.

Why would I write an entire chapter about staying in the school district when you are trying to move into EdTech? Simple – it's important to know your options. Many teachers – especially those newer to the field – have never really considered the options before them and think that the only real "promotions" within education happen when a teacher decides to become a dean, vice principal, or principal. Becoming an administrator is one option, but there are others. And moving into the EdTech world may take a lot longer than you think. In the meantime, how can you continue to grow professionally right where you are? I encourage you to read this chapter to explore this first path and take some notes as to what might be of interest to you.

For those of you reading this book who already *have* moved into different roles within your school district, you might skim this chapter or decide to read it for additional insights. For you too, it may take a long time to get that EdTech role you are thinking about, and finding a way to keep growing as you wait will be important.

I was speaking recently with a recruiter for an EdTech company, and I asked her what are some key traits she looks for when filling a role in an educational company. Her answer was very insightful. She stated that whenever a teacher tells her that they want to make a change because they do not see an opportunity to advance their career in education, that is a red flag. It shows her that they have not asked enough questions and explored the options available to them. If they have not grown in their own career path, then how can she trust that they will grow in another one?

With that in mind, it is essential that you continue to develop in your current career even while you explore other paths. Some of you will find an opportunity to transition into another role soon. For others, it could take months – even years. During that time, what can you do to grow? How can you develop in your current path?

The recruiter's advice was to start by asking questions. What do you *not* know about how education works? Do you know how new curriculum is adopted for your school? Do you know how purchasing works? Do you know how scheduling is done, how principals learn to fill out teacher evaluations, or how student records are transferred from one school to another? Do you know what steps are involved in Multi-Tiered Systems of Support to get students the support they need? Would you know how to coach another teacher, how your school budget works, or what the various laws are about school safety? Do you know exactly what your guidance counselor does, or your testing coordinator, instructional coach, or registrar? What does a day in their life look like?

I'll admit – I didn't know the answer to any of these questions when I was in the classroom. I was too busy with my own students. I was too busy asking how to get them to learn. But, I must admit, I also never really *thought* to ask these. They were someone else's job. And I wasn't even sure I *should* ask. I mean, everyone always seems so busy in schools.

But I would encourage you to be the one to ask these questions. Maybe not all at once, but the ones that really spark your interest – ask them! I don't know that there is any human being who doesn't want someone to take an interest in what they do. Many teachers love the relational part of their job – but we sometimes assume that professional rapport can only be established with our fellow teachers. Not so! Learn everything you can about the workings of your school. (Then, when you do decide to transition to an EdTech role, this knowledge will be a considerable asset for you as schools become your customers!)

Do you attend school board meetings? Do you volunteer to be a team leader? Do you ask for responsibility that you currently don't have?

I know that "volunteering" for more work as a teacher

doesn't seem wise or fair because the pay already is low, but hopefully you have seen in the last chapter that moving into another career doesn't actually guarantee a higher salary. And, in every step of my career, I was asked to do tasks that were not within my job description, and often I did these tasks outside of my regular work hours. This is not just a teaching thing; this is a *life* thing.

It is important to not lose sight of the opportunities you have *right now* to grow and learn. You may just discover that your next career path is right within your current organization!

What are some opportunities you may be interested in within the school system?

As we explore the different opportunities, I will provide the current average salary range for each position. These are average salaries in the United States at the time of writing, and all are provided by the U.S. Bureau of Labor Statistics. To provide a comparison to teaching, the current median salary for high school teachers in the United States is $62,870, while the median for elementary teachers is $60,660.[13] As discussed earlier, salaries vary widely, so I encourage you to compare the salaries for each position to the average teacher salary in your region to make a better educated decision.

*****

SCHOOL ADMINISTRATION

I know, I know. Right now, most of you reading this book are thinking, "I don't want to be a principal." My question is, why not? Your answers to that may not be reasons to actually avoid this position – or they might also help you determine what you *don't* want to do in a corporate position next. For example, if you don't want to be a school administrator because you don't want to pursue another degree, you may also limit yourself in the corporate world as some jobs that you might *love* may require another degree.

I would encourage you to sit down with your principal and assistant principal and ask, "What made you decide to pursue this position? What is a day in your life like? What do you love, and what do you dislike about being a school administrator?" The first thing to do is determine if you really have the right image of what it means to be a school administrator.

And don't just ask one principal! I would encourage you to share with your administrator that you want to consider what is next in your career – that you desire growth. And, if you don't get along with your principal, maybe make some calls during the summer to principals at nearby schools and ask if you can schedule 30 minutes of their time, and then ask *them*.

If you are an excellent communicator (not just in speaking but also in listening); a visionary; consistent and fair; able to balance praise with tough love towards both children *and* adults; organized and skilled with management; and a relationship builder, being a principal could be a fantastic position for you. Consider it! We need great administrators.

What about that requirement to pursue a master's degree (or *another* degree)?

For those of you who have not yet pursued a higher degree, I would highly recommend a degree in educational leadership. I do not have this, and even in my career outside of a school system, I find that this particular degree is often mentioned as a requirement or preference for a position I would love to consider. Even if you do not want to be a principal, consider expanding your education outside of the current content area you teach. For example, if you are a high school math teacher with a bachelor's degree in math, why pursue a master's in math? It won't earn you more as a *math* teacher. Unless you want to be considered for university math positions in the future, you may be better served by pursuing the educational leadership degree – or something else that will give you other opportunities.

How would a principal role compare to that of a teacher as far as salary? At this time, the national median salary for a principal is $98,490.[14] High school principals tend to make more than elementary school principals, but all make considerably more than classroom teachers.

*****

GUIDANCE COUNSELOR

If an educational leadership degree is not for you, you might find that a master's degree in school counseling is more to your liking. Guidance counselors have the ability to directly nurture and impact the lives of students in unique ways. Guidance counselors are able to focus on the social and emotional needs of students in ways teachers generally do not have the time for. Guidance counselors build key relationships with students and staff, and therefore the ability to build strong relationships and be an excellent listener and communicator are key characteristics of counselors.

In many ways, a guidance counselor serves as an all-around coach and cheerleader for students and staff. Responsibilities include helping students set and achieve academic or personal goals, develop social/emotional skills, and make behavioral modifications; supporting teachers with their students' educational progress; and assisting students and their families when facing difficult times or hardships, making referrals to other resources for help, and providing support with decisions about educational next steps.

Guidance counselors also have other tasks assigned to them outside of what might be considered their job description. Many guidance counselors find that they are called to serve as lunchroom or playground monitors or emergency substitute teachers, and may also be required to monitor detention, handle discipline, or support testing. The additional duties of a guidance counselor can increase levels of stress and frustration.

With the current focus on social and emotional learning, there is an increased demand for school counselors. In fact, the Bureau of Labor Statistics predicts that demand for school counselors will increase by 8% in the next decade, a rate described as "much faster than average." The current median salary for guidance counselors is $58,120.[15]

*****

SPECIALIZED FIELD

Education majors are specialized by grade level, and teachers start their career focusing on early childhood education, elementary grades, middle school or high school education. But there are additional areas of specialization that can be pursued. Depending on the specialization, you may or may not wish to add an education specialist degree, which typically is done after a master's degree. Why would you pursue one of those areas if you are trying to stop working in a classroom?

The answer is personal growth. Remember what the recruiter said about growth. If you tell a recruiter that you didn't have any opportunity for growth, and yet you have not pursued opportunities that *are* available to you, it reveals that you are not really a self-starter (a *big* buzzword among EdTech companies) or as driven as you might like to think. Plus, many of these specialized degrees will be an asset to you in the corporate world. If your transition out of the classroom is not happening as quickly as you would like it to and you find yourself in the classroom again, consider adding to your experience by taking classes or pursuing a degree in another area. Degrees in educational technology, adult learning, learning and development, instructional design, and curriculum and instruction all lead to future possibilities in education *and* the corporate world – and will certainly give you additional skills that can immediately apply to your own teaching.

How do you select a degree? Consider what you may want to do in the future. If you envision yourself serving as a professional learning consultant, consider specializing in educational leadership, adult learning, or instructional design. If you envision yourself working in EdTech, consider pursuing a degree in educational technology or even taking some business or marketing classes. Become a student of job postings and take notes on what areas of specialization are emphasized as required or even just preferred. Then begin by looking into classes in those areas.

Considering that many school districts will reimburse a certain number of credits each year, taking advanced courses towards a specialist's degree will go a long way to increasing your salary at the same time as you grow professionally. According to the National Council on Teacher Quality (NCTQ), 88% of large districts in the country increase a teacher's salary when they obtain a master's degree. "On average, a master's degree earns teachers an additional $2,760 in their first year of teaching compared to a bachelor's degree. This salary advantage expands to an average of $7,358 per year by the time a teacher reaches the maximum point of the pay scale," states the NCTQ.[16] Many districts continue to offer increases in salary for credits taken after obtaining a master's degree towards a specialist degree.

With the increased pay offered to those with specialist degrees, planning to complete your degree within two to four years will provide additional pay while in the classroom and give you the additional experience to help you stand out among a very crowded field of competitors in the corporate job market.

*****

INSTRUCTIONAL / MATH / LITERACY COACH

If you have been in the classroom for some time, an instructional coaching position is a valuable career move for anyone who is thinking about possibly working in education consulting in the future.

I learned more about how to be a good teacher by coaching *others* on high-leverage practices than I did in the classroom. This was mainly because I did not have an instructional coach working with me when I was teaching. For that reason, education for me was truly like working in a silo. I had no idea what others were doing, how they were teaching, and what practices they might be using that I wasn't. I also had limited feedback on what practices were working to engage all my students. Teachers spend most of the time alone with their students, which means it is very difficult for them to know for certain whether they are really an exceptional teacher. I honestly thought I was an exceptional teacher. But after 10 years in the classroom, I had the opportunity to coach. Coaching allowed me to observe many different teaching styles and classrooms, and for the first time in my teaching career, I got to see truly outstanding teachers engaging their students in ways I had never thought to.

Coaching was the most challenging thing I did in the school system, and the most powerful career move I made. When coaching, I read more books about great instruction than I had in college and graduate school. I then had the opportunity to apply what I was learning by observing teachers and providing feedback, and modeling strategies when needed. But the true essence of coaching comes not in the observing or the modeling, but in the conversation.

Coaching taught me how to work with adult learners. In coaching, I began to learn how to apply data analysis that leads to new practices, and then reflect on those practices and start the cycle all over again. I learned how to work with adult learners, coming alongside them and helping them reflect on their own data and determine what practices to adopt next based on their student goals. Good coaching is less about telling and more about listening, questioning, and reflecting.

The move to coaching was not an easy one, though, I must admit. There was always a quiet nagging voice in my head asking, "Who am I to try to help others be better teachers? Why should they trust me?" Honestly, sometimes those same questions would be spoken aloud by my colleagues. Coaching can be lonely in the sense that it puts you on a different plane than your colleagues. Not a higher plane – just a different one. Coaching is not meant to be evaluative, but depending on the school climate and the administrative leadership, coaches can be placed in a very difficult position between the teachers and the administration.

And yet, it was by stepping into the coaching role that I really grew in my professional practice. It was through coaching that I began to work in the district, learning from other coaches and having the opportunity to facilitate professional learning at the district level. It was through coaching that I was first exposed to how decisions about curricula or educational tools were made, and I had my first opportunity to interact with my district's educational executive leadership. All of these opportunities led to future opportunities that I had never even considered when I was in the classroom.

There is one thing I wish I had done differently as a coach, and for those of you who are already coaches, I want to encourage you in this area. I wish I had considered taking classes in adult learning while coaching. There are many free classes online if getting a degree in adult learning is not something you want to do. LinkedIn Learning®, for example, has courses in learning and development, facilitation and presentation skills, and instructional design. All of these would have helped me develop my skills even more as a coach. Instead, I spent all of professional learning time honing my teaching skills. This was great on the one hand, but to truly help my "clients" – the teachers I was working with – I would have benefitted from learning more about how adult learners are different and how to use my teaching gifts for a different audience in the most impactful way.

Becoming a coach in a district is often a lateral move in terms of salary, so coaching in and of itself will not necessarily result in a raise. However, it is a great opportunity to consider if you are looking for opportunities to grow within your career – and taking additional courses to help you work with adult learners *can* lead to additional pay. Also, coaching can give you key transferable skills to working in the corporate world of education. ZipRecruiter® reported an average national salary of $63,048 for instructional coaching.[17]

*****

CURRICULUM DEVELOPER

Curriculum developers are sometimes also referred to as curriculum specialists or instructional coordinators. Their key role is to oversee the curriculum at a school or district, develop instructional materials, ensure that the materials are implemented, and assess the effectiveness of materials being used. Their role can include some coaching but is often focused more on analyzing student data to determine gaps, assessing curriculum standards, and reviewing curriculum to ensure that standards are addressed in an accessible way. Training teachers on new curriculum or methods may also be included in the role.

Curriculum developers must enjoy researching new and different educational tools and curriculum and have an in-depth knowledge of the applicable educational standards to be able to determine a good fit. They must be analytical and have a desire to impact learning by seeking out the best curriculum for students. Often curriculum developers specialize in a certain area, by subject and even by grade level.

Curriculum developers are often hired at the district level or are shared between more than one school, and therefore some of their time is spent traveling between schools. Although they must be driven by a passion for working with children to improve education, they no longer are working in a classroom environment, and frequently have even less exposure to actual classrooms than instructional coaches, who often are school based. Curriculum developers are also employed, usually, for 12 months of the year and therefore have a higher base salary than teachers – but this can also vary depending on where the developer works. Not all curriculum developers work in a public-school setting. Those working for government agencies generally make more than those working for schools. And those working in postsecondary education make the least, according to Resilient Educator.[18] The median salary for curriculum developers is currently $66,970.[19]

If you currently are a curriculum developer looking to

transition into the educational corporate world, I again recommend honing your skills by taking classes in learning and development or instructional design. Many companies looking for instructional designers especially look for those with experience in software for designing eLearning or online courses, such as Storyline or Articulate 360. I highly recommend honing your skills and making yourself more marketable by becoming proficient in one of these areas. We will discuss this more in the last chapter.

*****

There are, of course, additional ways to grow as a professional in the education sector. They may or may not require additional degrees, but all are areas that, based on your interests and skills, you might wish to pursue. It is also important to consider each opportunity as a foot in the door. Most transitions do not happen easily, and with networking being the best way to land a job, pursuing opportunities when they present themselves is advisable so that you meet more people and can introduce them to your skills. Don't forget to consider how you might leverage your skills and expand your professional portfolio by looking into options such as:

- Becoming an adjunct professor at your local community college
- Serving as an interpreter if you are fluent in another language for school districts, educational centers or museums near you
- Working as an online tutor or even an overseas English teacher during your summer

Look at the careers page for your school district. Read all the openings and see what sparks your interest. Then analyze the prerequisite skills and begin to pursue those. I especially encourage those of you who are newer in the field to do this as, with less experience working in the district, you likely have a limited idea of the opportunities that are right in front of you. It may be that your next growth opportunity is within the district where you currently work.

*****

REFLECTION QUESTIONS

1. What have you done to grow in your profession right where you are?
2. What questions have you never thought to ask about how schools operate that ignite your curiosity?
3. Who can you pursue within your own school or district to learn more about how your school operates?
4. Which, if any, of the careers mentioned above sparked your interest? Why? What interests you about those positions? How can you learn more about opportunities to advance into those positions?
5. What can you do to pursue a next step in your career right where you are? What can you do that will be advantageous to you both in your current role and in the role you hope to attain?
6. List your current skills. Think about your communication skills, tech skills, presentation skills, etc. Which ones are easily transferable to a new role? What skills might you be lacking that you would be interested in developing?
7. Who can you tell in your own school or district about your desire to grow professionally? Try to think of people who will support your growth. Ask them to coffee and brainstorm ideas with them.

4

WHAT POSITIONS SHOULD I CONSIDER IN THE CORPORATE WORLD?

You wouldn't be reading this book if you were not at least considering making the move out of education entirely and into the corporate world. There is tremendous opportunity to develop your skills and talents in a completely new role now, with the incredible growth of the EdTech industry. But EdTech may not be the only area in which to look. Not all education companies are EdTech companies, and it's important to understand the difference.

So what exactly is EdTech, and how might EdTech companies be different from other companies that work with educators? EdTech businesses focus on creating ethical technologies that can be used by classroom teachers to support student engagement and learning and improve student performance. The primary goal of EdTech is to improve education by supporting the teaching and learning process using technology. Teachers can leverage technology to personalize learning and better capture data around student learning.

EdTech's growth has skyrocketed during the Covid-19

pandemic, but even prior to 2020 the outlook for the EdTech industry was glowing. According to an article published in *The Atlantic*, "The ed-tech market totaled $8.38 billion in the 2012-13 academic year."[20] By 2019, that value had increased almost tenfold, to $76.4 billion; in 2020, the market was valued at $89.49 billion, and is expected to have a compound annual growth rate of 19.9% through 2028, according to Grand View Research.[21]

You've likely experienced this growth personally in your classroom. Middle and high school classrooms often now encourage students to have cell phones with them so that students can take part in a quick online engagement survey or exit ticket. Teachers are now almost universally familiar with Learning Management Systems (LMSs), and, even pre-Covid, the majority of American teachers reported that they used digital learning tools with students every day – especially at the middle and high school levels – including online games, videos, websites, apps, online tutorials and other programs, according to a 2019 Gallup and New Schools Venture Fund report.[22]

All this growth means that there are a *lot* of opportunities for careers in the EdTech industry. *Prior* to the pandemic, a British study by Censuswide found that there were just under 1,400 EdTech companies *in the United States alone*, which made up slightly less than half of the global EdTech market.[23] To put that in perspective, there were approximately 130 hotel brands and just over 900 health insurance companies in the United States during the same year.[24]

If you are a tech-savvy teacher, have been using technology in your classroom, and believe in the power of technology to extend the role of the teacher, EdTech might be the perfect industry for your next career. However, not all teachers have found that the switch to digital modes of teaching and learning has been easy. They are disgruntled by technology and report that the prevalence of technology use in the classroom is one more reason for the stress that they feel on a regular basis. For these teachers, looking at other educational opportunities in the corporate world would be a good option.

Educational publishing is another area that many teachers consider. Educational publishing companies are the ones that produce the physical materials that you may be familiar with – everything from textbooks to trade books to study guides. Some of these physical components also come with a digital platform used in tandem with the curriculum. These companies are often seeking former teachers to help with content development and training on their specific curricula, and although there will certainly be some use of technology, it is not the sole focus of educational publishers. At the time of this writing, there are over 600 educational and academic publishing companies worldwide, according to Publishers Global.[25] Teachers will recognize some of them, such as McGraw-Hill, Pearson, Scholastic, Cengage Learning, and Houghton Mifflin Harcourt – the global "Big 5" educational publishers – but may be surprised to find other companies that have a far reach and/or specific area of focus that might interest them.

Another area in corporate America for teachers to consider is the world of corporate education. Corporate education, as I use the phrase, refers to the professional development needs of any corporation to ensure that employees receive proper training to do their job well. Sometimes this is referred to as learning and development. If you are comfortable working with adults and are willing to expand into adult education, a role within corporate education might be a great fit for you as well. The corporation may not specifically focus on education, and so you might find that you will need to prepare for a role like this by expanding your knowledge base into other areas – especially adult learning practices – but if you love teaching and can see yourself working with adults, this is certainly another booming industry in the corporate world.

Whether you choose to focus on EdTech, educational publishing, or branching out into adult learning in other areas of the corporate world, one of the best places to start is to understand the types of roles available to you. What are the different jobs that teachers often transition into? What are their requirements and prerequisite skills? And how do you know which ones might be the best for you? That will be the focus of the remainder of this chapter.

Let's now turn our attention to the different types of jobs that many educators consider applying for in the corporate world.

*****

CUSTOMER SUCCESS MANAGER

Recently I have seen a trend on social networking sites of current and former teachers posting that they are looking to become a customer success manager. I find it interesting that this seems to be almost exclusively the job title that teachers are looking for. It makes me wonder if they really understand what a customer success manager does and what else might be available. There are numerous posts that the customer success position is the "entry level" position for teachers, or comments that these positions are the easiest for educators to get. That may not be the case! Although this position is a great one to consider, it may not be a good fit for all teachers, and depending on your gifts and skills, it may not be as natural a fit as other roles could be.

First and foremost, it is important to understand what is meant by "customer success." It might first be beneficial to say what customer success is *not*. Customer success is *not* the same as customer *service* or *support*. Customer service and support teams help customers understand how their product works and support the customer when there are any product-related issues. They usually focus on the technological side of an EdTech platform and solve "tech issues."

Customer *success* is different. According to the Customer Success Association, customer success refers to a "long-term, scientifically engineered, and professionally directed business strategy for maximizing customer and company sustainable proven profitability." Customer success is about retaining customers – keeping a company's customers happy so that they will continue to purchase goods and/or services from that company, expanding into new products and services whenever possible. Customer success is "an integration of functions and activities of marketing, sales, professional services, training and support into a new profession."[26]

There are a couple of things to unpack with that statement. First of all, customer success is a fairly new profession. Although there certainly are people who have several years of experience in customer success, very few people have decades of experience. Customer success, as a specific role and function of a company, only dates back to the late 1990s when a company called Vantive created the very first customer success department, and it wasn't until around 2004–2005 that other companies began to follow suit as they began to see how ensuring that a customer is successful ultimately meant that they would profit more since the satisfied customer would renew the subscription for their product.[27]

What this means for you as an inexperienced customer success manager is that you do not need to dwell on your lack of experience. Many customer success managers are fairly new to the role. Instead, you should focus on learning what a customer success manager does and then think about how your background and skills will enable you to excel at this role.

Great EdTech customer success managers (CSMs) need to have a deep understanding of three key things: their customers' needs, the product itself, and the field of education. As an educator, you already have a deep understanding of the field of education and likely can more easily understand the overall goals of the customer over someone with years of experience as a CSM in a domain other than education. So, don't undervalue what you bring to the table. You have at least two of the three key pillars of a great EdTech customer success manager already, and becoming a product expert is something you would be able to do once hired by the company.

The second point to unpack in the statement about customer success is what a customer success manager's end goal is. Yes, the goal is to make sure your customers are happy and successful with using the product. But it is not *just* about that. Companies want happy customers who will then return to their product and purchase again, and more than last time. A customer success manager's job is, ultimately, to ensure that the organization they are supporting is successful *so that the company makes revenue*. Another way to say this is that a customer success manager's job is to decrease "churn" – or the number of customers cancelling their service or use of a company's product. As a matter of fact, the mission statement of customer success, as written by the Customer Success Association, is "to increase sustainable *proven* profitability for both the Customers *and* the Company."

Some people might balk at this mission, thinking that it seems greedy and manipulative for a company to "pretend" to care about the customer for the sole purpose of making money. That is a completely jaded and imbalanced way to think about this, however. A company that provides a product or a service must keep up with customer demands. They need to increase their ability to service customers, even as educational standards change, and even as the technology is constantly evolving. They need to pay the salaries of their employees. They need to be profitable to succeed and sustain their business over a long period of time. So, companies are not "pretending" to care about their customers. Instead, great companies have a very balanced understanding that when their customers are happy and successful, that is the best way for them to succeed as well. As companies learn from their customers' input and pivot to meet customers' evolving needs, they make their products better and better. A symbiotic relationship is formed, and there is success on both sides. As companies experience success, they should continue to increase their customers' success rate and happiness. Only then will the business continue to grow and do well.

Reducing churn, then, might be the easiest way to summarize the goal of a customer success manager. But it doesn't stop there. Customer success managers don't just react to unhappy customers by trying to solve problems. They also try to make every interaction with a customer one where trust is built and customers want to keep working with the company. Instead of reactive, the best customer success managers are proactive as well.

Ultimately…

The goal of a customer success manager is to sustain growth and profitability for the company.

How a customer success manager does this is by helping their customers successfully meet their goals.

There are a number of ways that customer success managers might do this, depending on the company. CSMs often are the ones asking the customer right away, "What is your goal for this product/service?" and "How will you know if you are having success with this product?" Right from the start, the customer success manager seeks to understand what each customer values and desires, and then will do everything they can to ensure that the customer finds that value. This can include working with the design and development teams to create new features requested by customers. It can mean working with the sales team to ensure they know of possible expansion opportunities or working with marketing teams to design campaigns that speak to a wider audience of customers. It often involves onboarding and training customers, and in the EdTech world, that also includes learning a great deal about the numerous Learning Management Systems (LMSs) and Student Information Systems (SISs) to be able to support customers (and may include doing some one-the-spot triage of technical issues). It almost certainly involves the ability to collect, track, and analyze data to ensure that the customer has the best experience possible.

It also involves challenging conversations. In the EdTech world, most products and services are purchased as a subscription. This is what is meant by SaaS, or "Software as a Service." Most EdTech products today are purchased via this model, where the software is not purchased with a perpetual license and downloaded on individual computers, but rather is purchased as a subscription for a period of time and accessed via the internet. This allows a school to benefit from ongoing upgrades and support from the EdTech company, and it mutually benefits the EdTech company, which is then able to sustain its profits over time as customers renew their subscription annually.

This is where customer success managers must be OK with having somewhat challenging conversations. Each spring, it is the customer success manager who calls current partnering schools and districts to ask them if they plan to renew their subscription, sends them invoices, and then continues to follow up until the invoices are paid. They are the ones who answer questions like, "Why does this product cost so much?" or "Why are you increasing your price?" They also take the calls or respond to the emails of customers who are dissatisfied or unhappy. They have to faithfully pursue the customers who avoid their calls or ignore their emails and maintain patience and professionalism when customers respond in unexpected or even unpleasant ways. (Even when a company is delivering a fantastic product or service and does all it can to be responsive to a customer's need, there are always going to be disgruntled individuals that a customer success manager must work with.)

A good question to ask about any position is, how will I be evaluated? As a customer success manager, your KPIs will generally relate to the overall goal of profitability. Your KPIs might include decreasing churn rates. Another might be increasing the customer lifetime value - the estimated amount of revenue a customer brings to a business during their entire relationship with them – by either increasing the customer's retention rate or increasing the amount of money they spend through upsells and expansion. A third possible KPI is having a certain Net Promoter Score (NPS). The NPS is generated by *just one question* asked to a customer. That one question is "How likely are you to recommend our product/service to others?" The customer answers on a scale of 1 to 10, with 1 meaning not at all likely and 10 meaning definitely likely. A response of 1–5 is not good. Those customers are considered detractors. A response of 6–8 is neutral. The desired response is 9–10. Those are the promoters who become your company's advocates. The

NPS is calculated by subtracting the percentage of detractor responses from the percentage of promotor responses. So, one KPI as a customer success manager might simply be your overall Net Promoter Score.

There are other possible KPIs for customer success managers. However, this gives you a sense of what type of expectations might be placed on you in this role.

As far as salary, the range is quite wide. Depending on the company, a CSM may have a lower base salary and then be given a monthly, quarterly, or annual bonus as they meet their KPIs. As of 2021, the median reported salary for customer success managers is $58,790, but that figure jumps to $64,290 when bonuses are included.[28] (The average salary varies greatly by state, however, with a difference of over $25,000 between the highest paying state, Massachusetts, and the lowest, Mississippi.)[29]

So is customer success the right fit for you? Do you feel comfortable working in a role where you will not only be training customers but also be laser-focused on doing all you can do to *ensure that they continue to purchase* your company's product? Are you comfortable having challenging conversations with school or district decision makers? Are you able to balance your desire to support teachers with the goal of ensuring that your company is profitable?

If so, then customer success might be a great fit for you! (Be sure to read the Customer Success Interview Questions in the appendix to help you prepare.) If not, though, perhaps another role might be a better choice.

*****

IMPLEMENTATION SPECIALIST/MANAGER

A role that is very similar to a customer success manager is an implementation specialist or implementation manager. This role may also be called onboarding manager or client onboarding specialist. Both the implementation team (where the implementation specialist focuses) and the success team (where the customer success manager focuses) make up the overall "customer experience" (CX). This refers to everything the customer experiences while working with your company, from initial exploration, through purchase, to implementation and continued usage or partnership.

First impressions matter. The implementation team is the group of specialists who make sure that customers who have purchased a company's product or service have an incredible "onboarding" experience. They want the customer to have a great first impression of the service and the company's commitment to them, and do everything they can to make sure this happens. Then, after the initial onboarding, the implementation specialist hands off the customer to the customer success manager. So, in brief, the implementation specialist focuses on the initial onboarding for a specific period of time and then gracefully hands off the customer to the customer success manager who will continue to foster the customer relationship, with the goal of retaining that customer over time.

How does an implementation specialist ensure a smooth and efficient onboarding experience? Excellent implementation specialists will be very focused, sequential, organized and detail oriented to enable the most productive onboarding experience for their customers.

An implementation specialist working for an EdTech company might support the customer (in this case, schools and districts) with rostering students and staff members and provide beginning training for customers. Having a background in various Learning Management Systems may give you an edge with this role (although it may not be required, so check the job description). Understanding Learning Tools Interoperability (LTI) is also beneficial. Although this may sound daunting, most teachers who have been working in a classroom recently have experience with both areas, even though they may never have paid attention to these actual terms before. (Basically, if you logged onto some platform in your classroom from which you could post assignments, access a gradebook, and launch other sites or learning tools and apps, you have experience with *both* an LMS and LTI.)

Implementation specialists identify the goals and priorities of the school or district's executive team so that customer success knows what to track over time to show the effectiveness of the solution they purchased. They are proactive, making sure to anticipate questions or challenges and formulating strategies and plans to make sure that the customer remains excited about using the product.

Implementation specialists are also very detail oriented. Because they know they are setting the stage for success with the customer, they work to ensure a cohesive experience for their customer. When they hand off the customer to the success manager, they do not want the customer to feel as if they are starting over, needing to restate their goals or preferences. Therefore, an excellent implementation specialist keeps careful notes after each conversation with the customer and has a plan for sharing that information in advance of the handoff to the customer success team.

Implementation specialists are working toward a given end date. All the onboarding tasks that are needed for a successful customer experience must be completed by a certain date, at which point the customer will be handed over to the customer success team. Therefore, although KPIs for an implementation specialist might be very similar to those for customer success, they may also involve project tracking measures such as percentage of tasks completed by the projected date.

Discerning the median or average salary of implementation specialists can be tricky as it varies by industry. In general, the average salary is around $60,000 (somewhat lower according to Glassdoor® and somewhat higher according to Indeed®) but the median salary is closer to $70,000.[30]

*****

CONSULTANT

Have you ever had the experience as a teacher of having someone from a company come to your classroom, observe you teaching, and then support you in some way (either through conversation, training, co-teaching, or modeling)? These are the people in consulting roles. They might work for an EdTech or educational publishing company, or they might be from another agency. They have many different titles – educational consultant, services consultant, professional services consultant, regional consultant – but they all support the customer (teachers, school leaders, and districts) directly with improving strategies, processes, policies, or use of a particular product to meet a stated overall objective, such as increasing literacy rates or decreasing dropout rates.

The consultants I am referring to are those that work for a specific education company and focus their consulting work on the curricula or products provided by that company. Sometimes these consultants can be referred to as educational consultants, but there is an entirely other branch of educational consulting that I am *not* focusing on. These are the independent educational consultants whose role is mostly helping students and their families navigate the opportunities available in higher education by providing guidance on colleges and admissions. Instead, the consultants I am referring to, whether they work for a company or independently, are those focused on supporting teachers, schools, and districts with meeting their goals for student success.

Consultant roles overlap in some ways with those of the customer success manager. Both the consultant and the customer success manager are focused on the customer (in this case the schools and districts hiring them) having success with the product they have purchased from the company. One key difference, though, is that the customer success manager is much more involved in making sure that the company is profitable because of the success of the customer. The customer success manager thinks about the customer *and* the company success. The consultant is often focused on ensuring that the customer succeeds in a very practical way and specifically, that the product or service the school or district purchased is meeting the specific goals of that organization by seeing tangible results in student achievement. Where the CSM might focus more on ensuring that the decision-maker (and "purse-holder") sees the overall value, the consultant generally works much more directly with the classroom teachers.

Consulting positions are the ones many teachers first think about when they consider leaving the classroom. They envision themselves in a career where they can coach teachers, provide professional development and support schools and districts in numerous ways. Consultants are the ones teachers see the most – the ones who do the initial or advanced training on a particular product or curriculum (although, depending on the company, these trainings may also be done by the customer success team), the ones who schedule meetings with them and coach them on a particular area of focus, or the ones who model the use of the curriculum or platform with the teacher's students in their classroom.

The consulting business was thriving in America prior to Covid-19. Many companies encouraged (or, in some cases, bundled) "services" to be sold with their products. Schools or districts would purchase a new curriculum or EdTech platform and be provided with services (embedded into the overall price of the curriculum), including initial training and in-person or online coaching services or advanced professional learning sessions. Then, in mid-March 2020, consulting came to a sudden stop as schools closed their doors. In-person consulting services were suspended, and companies had to pivot overnight to finding ways to support teachers with *online* services even as the teachers were navigating the transition to online teaching. Teachers quickly found that companies began offering services to support them with this sudden transition, and companies shifted into high gear as many of them who had never consulted or trained virtually in the past now had to coach and train others on how to teach online! During 2020–2021, many consultants were let go as demand for in-person consulting disappeared and companies found that they could service teachers remotely with fewer consultants who were no longer spending time traveling from place to place.

Prior to 2020, however, consulting was a prime area for teachers who wanted to leave the classroom and break into the corporate world of education – and it likely will regain momentum in the future (even if in-person services are not as much in demand). Schools and districts as well as educational companies now have, for the most part, successfully navigated to online support – and online coaching and training of teachers is becoming more the norm. (In many cases, companies charge so much more for in-person services that schools and districts opt for virtual services, even if in-person is favored.)

Professional services consultants are considered experts in their field. Many companies looking to hire consultants seek individuals with at least five years of experience as an educator. In most cases, a master's degree is required, as well as experience with leading teachers either as a team leader, instructional coach, administrator, or in some other way. Specialization is often helpful in the area of consulting, as many consultants will work with specific grade levels or subject areas – and those with educational leadership degrees and experience often are sought after to support school or district administrators. Consultants are familiar with the latest research and best practices in education and have the ability to communicate and teach these to teachers and administrators in a professional, empathetic and approachable manner.

What does the day in the life of a consultant look like? That will vary a great deal from one company to the next and will especially look different for those who are doing in-person visits versus those who work with teachers online. In general, consultants focus on helping schools or districts reach short- or long-term goals. A consultant may meet with school or district administrators to review and analyze current data and help them set or communicate their goals for students and/or teachers. The consultant usually provides initial and ongoing training on the program or curriculum to help teachers increase overall student achievement. The consultant may deliver leadership training as well. They meet with teachers or school leaders to provide coaching support, observe teachers in action, model for the teacher, and document progress toward goals. They often review student artifacts and data with individual teachers or departments and facilitate discussion on next steps toward the overall goal. By helping the customer be successful and maximize the use of the program, the consultant helps the customer see the value of the program, which leads to renewals.

What might surprise many teachers is the amount of work a consultant does *outside* of the classroom. The reporting and documentation of each delivered service for each teacher can be quite time-consuming. The consultant must keep meticulous notes and records of their visits and provide reports to the teachers and leaders they support to document progress toward the goals over time. Many companies require that these reports be shared with the customer within 24-48 hours of having met with them. So, after a long day meeting with teachers and leaders, consultants often spend their evenings writing reports.

I am often asked if consulting is something teachers could do as a second job – perhaps over the summer. Although there may be exceptions, in general, the answer is no. A consultant's busiest time of year is late summer through January as that is when many schools need training and consulting support and when teachers are back working in their classrooms. During the early summer months, most consultants spend their time preparing and doing internal work (although there may be some training opportunities as well.)

Professional services consultants are not involved in sales. They support the customer *after* the sale is made. However, they will still need to be aware of those soft upsell opportunities and communicate those to their sales partners. For example, if you are consulting for a company that provides a core ELA curriculum to a school district and discover in your coaching and consulting work that they have a high population of students who struggle with reading, you might suggest to them that they also consider purchasing your company's supplemental intervention curriculum to support these students – and then you let the sales partner know about this deficit so that they can follow up.

The best professional services consultants in education are those who have several years of experience in teaching, and possibly are specialized in a particular area. Consultants are often considered the Subject Matter Expert (SME – pronounced in the business world like "Smee"). Great consultants enjoy working with adults and are comfortable under pressure. They must be excellent facilitators and be able to read their audience and engage adult learners in meaningful dialogue and discussion. They must be highly skilled at active listening, asking probing questions and identifying challenges and concerns that a teacher or administrator might only be hinting at. They must be excellent communicators, both orally and in writing. And they must have a high degree of emotional intelligence. Consultants work on a daily basis with teachers who are, as you know, under extreme amounts of stress. Therefore, consultants need to be able to balance the need to show support and care with the goal of increasing student or teacher performance. This can be tricky. Not all teachers *want* to be coached. (In my career as a consultant, it was rare that a teacher embraced coaching right from the start.) Therefore, an excellent consultant is one with expertise in the field but also with the humility to know they must gain their clients' trust and respect– clients who are, often, worn out and therefore not the most receptive.

A professional services consultant also has to meet KPIs and targets. These will vary by company and job description. One KPI might relate to how many services you delivered, be it in hours or days. You may have a specific target of hours or days that you will be required to deliver. Another

KPI might relate to customer satisfaction surveys for services delivered and Net Promoter Scores, similar to a customer success manager.

However, it is important to keep in mind that although you do not directly bring in revenue, the overall goal of the company continues to be sustained profitability. Therefore, even if your KPIs do not mention revenue, you will want to find out how the company determines the value you personally bring to the company and meet or exceed those expectations. During difficult times (like the pandemic) when companies need to decrease their professional services workforce, the survey ratings from trainings delivered may not matter as much as the amount of revenue you generated by delivering a higher number of services than expected. Seek to understand the company's overall strategy for increasing revenue, and then learn how you can contribute to that goal. This may not be something you expect in a role where you are focused on working with teachers and not doing direct sales, but when hard times hit, a company looks at their finances and determines who is best supporting their overall goal of profitability. You want to be that person!

Professional services consultants are less likely than others in education companies to receive a bonus. Rather, they often have a higher base salary. The median base salary for a professional services consultant in the United States is currently $70,080 – with this salary again varying by location and also industry.[31] (It is important to note that the median salary is likely more appropriate to consider than the average. Average consultant salaries are reported at $83,450 – but this number is greatly swayed by the salaries of the top 5% of consultants, which approach $200,000.[32] Keep in mind, though, that consultants work in every sector, and those that work with computers or in other higher-paying industries are the ones making closer to that figure.)

*****

CONTENT WRITER

Many educational companies post jobs looking for "content writers." Content writing can be an excellent area for former teachers with great written communication skills to explore.

Content writing jobs may fall into two areas: educational content/instructional design and marketing. As a teacher, being an educational content writer is where you can leverage teaching experience to make a difference by reaching a larger number of students and teachers. If you are the kind of teacher who found yourself writing lesson plans that then were shared across your entire team, you might enjoy being an educational content writer. Content writing roles focused on marketing are more about company's presence and may require additional training in the area of marketing. For this reason, I will focus on educational content writing. In this section, we will consider those positions that create educational content consumed by teachers and students, while the next section will look at instructional design roles.

Educational content writers create all sorts of educational content for both teachers and students. They outline curriculum, research best practices and strategies, and write the content for learning materials that are then sold to schools for use with their students. Content writers might help with writing a teacher's guide or digital resources, test questions, or study guides.

What makes a great educational content writer, aside from the ability to effectively communicate in written form? First, educational experience. Educational content writers must have a deep understanding of the importance of engaging students with great content. They must be able to relate concepts in a clear way for the targeted ages and levels of students as well as take a culturally responsive approach that considers their different backgrounds. Educational content writers must have a sense of how long something might take to teach, what the constraints of the classroom likely are, and how a teacher could differentiate the material in the lesson plan for different students, such as English learners or those ready for a challenge. Educational content writers must be able to analyze the standards that a teacher must teach and then write meaningful and engaging content that will specifically support students' learning of those standards. They create curricula, assessments, and courses around content in a way that intentionally incorporates broad frameworks, including depth of knowledge, universal design of learning, Bloom's taxonomy, and culturally responsive education – all while making the content rigorous *and* relevant to students.

Of course, educational content writers also need to be excellent communicators with a firm grasp of style and grammar. They need to be able to research, plan, draft, revise and edit their content in a timely manner, meeting deadlines and adjusting their writing to remain relevant based on ever-evolving standards and educational research and expectations. Research ability is of paramount importance to good writers. Content writers should *enjoy* research (as it is a critical part of their job) and must be able to ferret out the reliable sources of information from the sea of digital content. They must be able to stay abreast of current trends and thought leaders by monitoring blogs, journals, and twitter posts.

Additionally, content writers must be open to feedback and willing to change their writing style. As one content writer expressed to me, "It's not the type of writing where you get a byline and make it your own. It needs to have a common voice/style, and you have to be willing to get feedback." Then, you must be able to act on that feedback in a way that allows your writing to blend and flow with one voice, contributed by possibly many different individuals.

Many content writers do not start with full-time work. A scan of job boards will quickly reveal that content writers are often hired on a part-time, contract, or freelance basis. The development process, and therefore the need for content writers, is not steady. There might be a lot of content writers needed for a new program launching, but once the content is written, the need declines. (However, one content writer shared that this may be changing with the move toward ongoing digital content updates and releases as part of the SaaS model.)

The demand for part-time content writers can be a good thing for teachers with time to do some work on the side and take a "foot in the door" approach to this type of work. Should one land a full-time position, though, the median salary for writers in 2020 was $67,120, although this may be significantly lower depending on the content you are being asked to write. Content writing jobs are also predicted to decline over the next decade, although those in the field argue that the need for content writing may not *decline* as much as *change*.[33] Instead of writing traditional content for text books or lesson plans, for example, there will be an increasing need for content designed for digital-first consumption. In any case, be prepared for lots of competition for jobs if you plan to pursue this as a field. That is another reason that starting with some part-time or freelance work might be a good option for you as it will provide valuable experience needed to stand out on a resume.

Although it may be discouraging to think that getting a full-time content writing job will be difficult, if this is an area that interests you, start now! Consider all the lessons you currently write. Are you sharing content with your team? If so, consider sharing it online as well. Start an educational blog focusing on a specific topic or audience to build your writing credibility. Look for educational magazines that accept article submissions. There are many ways that you can break into content writing as a freelancer, independent writer, or contract writer – and this is valuable experience for transitioning into a career in writing later. You can begin to seek out freelance positions by searching specifically for them, of course, but you can also join online communities where freelance writers advertise their services and can get connected with potential employers. Upwork (www.upwork.com) is an example of one online community for writers.

Another reason to start working as a part-time freelance content writer is that if you apply to a full-time position as a content writer, you will almost certainly be required to submit samples of your writing. These should be writing samples published in print or online and should be related to the type of writing you are applying for. For example, if you are applying for a position as a content writer focusing on elementary STEM, you don't want to send samples of your personal blog.

No matter what type of content writing job you apply for, it is likely that you will be asked to complete some sort of writing test or task as part of your interview process. This is to ensure that you are a good fit for the company's needs. On several occasions, I have seen job searchers online post that this type of "task" is a way for the company to get someone to complete a job for free. It isn't. It is a necessary task to ensure that the applicant truly can deliver what they say they can and should be taken very seriously. You demonstrate your ability to *research* as well as write during this test because they can evaluate what you know about the company, the field, and the writing process through this one assignment. If you spell their company name wrong, don't know their target audience, or can't communicate the content in a similar style to what they need, you will not be hired. Do your research about the company in advance of this task.

A content writer's performance will be evaluated on the writing they produce, of course, but it is also important to remember that return on investment (ROI) is always a component of how someone is evaluated in the corporate world. Content writers will certainly need to meet deadlines and produce a certain number of articles or a specific number of digital posts within a given timeframe. Educational content writers will be evaluated on the quality of the content they produce within the specified timeframe, as well as their ability to act on feedback. (In contrast, content writers focused on marketing will likely be evaluated in part by the views and comments on content they create, or by the amount of traffic generated by their work. The keys are traffic and engagement. If readers are brought to the content – and engage in the content – and if that content results in sales leads, the content writer is providing value to the company.)

For this reason, it will be important to consider the specific type of writing that the content writer is being asked to produce. If the role is strictly creating content for teachers to use in the classroom, that will be evaluated in one way. If the position includes creating content for the business's online presence, that will require another set of skills and be evaluated in a different way – hence the need for possibly learning some marketing strategies if you decide to pursue a content writer position that focuses on driving users to your company's site.

*****

INSTRUCTIONAL DESIGNER

Closely related to content writing positions are those of instructional designers. Have you ever taken a LinkedIn Learning® course or other online course to improve your skills in a specific area? These courses are created by instructional designers. Instructional designers use their educational and technological expertise to address gaps in learning and ensure outcomes for the learners. Instructional designers work independently or with teams of people (including SMEs) to design video tutorials, games, simulations, instructional manuals, and online courses that will effectively identify the learning gaps and fill them. Instructional design (ID) might also be termed Instructional Systems Design (ISD) and will likely also mention terms like "educational technology" and/or "curriculum development."

One difference between instructional designers and curriculum developers is that instructional designers focus on adult, professional learning. Curriculum developers often focus on teaching materials and making sure materials align to standards. Another key difference between an instructional designer and a curriculum developer is that the designer will almost always be using technology to meet the learning needs, often delivered in an asynchronous format, while a curriculum developer, depending on where they work, may be creating more lessons for in-person delivery. Teachers who love learning and using technology to address gaps in student learning might love to transition into the role of an instructional designer.

As a side note, Learning Experience Design (LX, or LX

Design) is another field that is related to instructional design and is sometimes used interchangeably. LX is a newer field and tends to focus more on *product development and design* aspects of the learner's experience. Depending on whether you are speaking with an instructional designer or a learning designer, you will hear differences of opinion about how much these positions overlap. If you apply for an LX position, I recommend asking questions of the interviewer about how they view this role and whether they view LX and ID as the same or different. They may make a definite distinction between the two, or they may be using the terms interchangeably. I will focus on instructional design roles unless I specifically state differently.

Instructional design is a great fit for many teachers, but one usually cannot step directly into this role from a classroom. It is important that instructional designers have an excellent understanding of how to address the learning needs of adults, who differ in their learning process needs than younger individuals. Adult learning theory, or "andragogy," was defined by Malcolm Knowles, an American educator who attempted to delineate the differences between adult and child learners. According to Knowles' theory of andragogy, adults learn best when they:

1. Have a clear understanding of *why* they need to learn something and are involved in planning their instruction and the methods of evaluating their learning.
2. Learn by experience, including allowing them to learn from their mistakes.
3. Use the learning to solve a problem rather than memorize or relate new content.
4. Believe the learning is relevant to them and that it will bring them immediate value in their personal or work lives.

Any learning experience created for adults should therefore allow the learner to identify their own learning goals and select the content that will best help them meet these goals – and ensure that they can immediately apply this learning to their situation. The adult learner must *buy in* to the learning experience for it to be of value to them.

One key difference between a *teacher* and an *instructional designer* is that instructional designers are not always masters of the content they are creating. Many instructional designers will work closely with an individual or team of SMEs who have a much better grasp of the content itself. The instructional designer is not always expected to become a SME themselves, but rather to identify, by working closely with the SMEs, what learners truly need to understand and how to get them to that point. Therefore, being an excellent listener and communicator is a key skill for instructional designers.

Another difference between being a teacher and an instructional designer is that the instructional designer is not always the person *delivering* the content. They *might* be, but not always. Sometimes the person delivering the content is the corporate trainer (but more on that below). The designer, rather, is most often the one who uses a specific model to decide what learning gaps need to be addressed, determines how to address those gaps, and then creates content to do just that. Then, after implementing the content, the instructional designer determines what changes need to be made to improve the learning outcomes.

Instructional design jobs often specify a model that their designers will use to identify the learning gaps, design the course and materials that will address these gaps, create a method to evaluate learning, and analyze the results to ensure that the course is effective. Although there are a number of different instructional design methods, two of the most common include ADDIE and SAM. ADDIE (an acronym for Analyze, Design, Development, Implementation, Evaluation) continues to be the most widely used model, but SAM (Successive Approximation Model) is becoming more and more popular as well. SAM allows for a quicker design and analysis process than ADDIE. If you are interested in instructional design, both models will be important to understand and implement. (This is one difference between instructional design and learner experience design. An LX designer generally utilizes *design* processes, not ADDIE or SAM. If a job description for an LX designer mentions ADDIE or SAM, you can assume that the company views these two roles as synonymous – although I would still recommend asking about that.)

Becoming an instructional designer means committing to constantly learning. Because instructional designers are expected to use technology to meet the needs of their learners, they must keep current with ever-evolving technology. And, as new learning theories are created and introduced, instructional designers need to keep abreast of these as well. However, it may not be necessary to get an advanced degree in instructional design. Instructional design or educational technology degrees are often required for employment at a school district or university, but companies looking to hire instructional designers often do not require degrees and instead place more emphasis on work experience.[34]

When asked what she looks for when hiring an instructional designer from the classroom, one director of content writing at an educational company shared with me that the main thing she looks for is "experience designing learning for adult learners" often through facilitation of site-based professional development within a school or district. She wrote, "I've seen candidates who don't do this full time but might be a lead teacher or have volunteered to lead sessions. I'll ask to see samples, in this case often [a PowerPoint], to see how they design the learning experience. Are there objectives or outcomes, a clear agenda, opportunities to interact, process and apply learning, etc.? I have found that just because someone is a strong teacher, it does not necessarily mean they are aware of how best to design adult learning. On the flip side, though, as teachers they have been on the receiving end of professional development and often have an idea of what works and what doesn't."

How is an instructional designer evaluated? One instructional designer I spoke with shared that at her company, performance evaluation included customer survey feedback but also considered the designer's ability to meet deadlines, be innovative and open to feedback, and collaborate with SMEs and other product team members. However, evaluation methods will vary from one position to another and one company to another. Generally, an instructional designer's performance will be evaluated in some way by looking at the outcomes of the course they created. Did the learners effectively learn what the course set out to teach them? In many ways, this type of evaluation is likely the most familiar to teachers who are used to being evaluated by their students demonstrating what they have learned. An instructional designer's evaluation may include learners' survey results about what they learned and whether or not they liked the course. Some companies strictly focus on the training aspects of the instructional designer – how many courses were developed, how many employees took the course, whether participants enjoyed the course, etc.

I recommend that if you do land a position as an instructional designer and have the opportunity to create your own KPIs, you look beyond these targets. The reason is that, although these aspects are incredibly important for you to consider as an instructional designer, they do not necessarily equate to a return on investment (ROI) for the business. The business leaders need to see that they are either saving money or making money when employees take your course. How many employees you trained or courses you wrote mean very little if there is no obvious ROI.

For this reason, the KPIs of instructional designers should (or already do) include measurable outcomes that affect the business's bottom line. For example, a course for sales representatives should result in increased sales, which can be monitored with data and tracked over time. Other courses might increase work outflow or decrease time on task or error rates. As with any good instruction, IDs begin with the end in mind – and the end of the course should result in ROI for the company. That promised ROI should be measurable in some way. A good instructional designer will work to identify the gaps the company currently has and improvements that could be made, and then design courses specifically with that end in mind. For more information on this, visit eLearning Industry's online forum.[35]

The average base salary of an instructional designer is between \$65,000 and \$70,000 and may include a bonus, but that is less common in this field.[36] After Covid, many instructional designers work remotely, not from an office, so your location may not influence your pay as much. If you are given the opportunity to negotiate your salary, you may want to consider whether the company pays based on location or job title. According to Glassdoor®, location-based pay will provide a salary based on the cost of living for your area.[37] This can be great if you live in a city with a high cost of living. However, if the salary is based on the job itself, it will tend to be more in line with the average salaries across the United States, meaning everyone at the company with that job title is paid about the same. Neither of these is definitely more advantageous. It will depend on where you live and what your needs are for your living expenses.

*****

CORPORATE TRAINER

Another role that relates closely to instructional design is corporate training. The easiest way to explain the difference between these two roles is to think of the instructional designer as the one who *creates* the course or material to be delivered, while the corporate trainer is the one to actually *deliver* the course or training session. They can overlap, though, depending on the role, so one should always read the job descriptions carefully and ask about this during an interview.

Much like professional services consultants or instructional coaches, corporate trainers are much more involved in direct instruction of adults. Corporate trainers are teachers, but their target audiences are employees who work for an organization. Corporate trainers are experts in adult learning theory, much like instructional designers, but are often tasked more with delivering the content rather than designing the content. They may work solely for one large company or firm, or they may work for a consulting organization that partners with many different companies. Some established or niche trainers may work independently as freelancers.

Corporate training positions can seem like an easy move for classroom teachers. After all, corporate trainers are teachers! However, not all teachers are comfortable working with adult learners, so it may not be the right position for everyone. Being a corporate trainer involves teaching expertise, certainly, but it also involves knowledge of the field in which you are training, as corporate trainers are employed by organizations across industries – from construction to retail to legal services to hospitals. In fact, one way to increase your likelihood of getting a position as a corporate trainer is to identify a field in which you have other experience or expansive interest and focus on getting a position as a trainer in that market.

Corporate trainers also are experts in communication and public speaking, but corporate training is *not* the same as giving a keynote address. Although a corporate trainer may speak to a very large group of participants or attendees, learner engagement is still necessary, including providing tasks such as role-playing activities and giving feedback. Corporate trainers must be able to read their audience and communicate effectively with large groups.

Just like in the classroom, corporate trainers need to be flexible and adaptable. There will be times where a corporate trainer expects a session to be filled with people of a certain experience level only to discover that the audience is mostly far less experienced, or far more! There will be situations where activities that worked well in the past do not apply, or when questions are asked that are completely unexpected. Excellent corporate trainers have skills that allow them to adapt to the moment while still delivering the expected outcomes of the course.

Corporate trainers most definitely need to be empathetic to their learners. They need to understand possible frustration points and be prepared to overcome resistance. That is why the best corporate trainers have a firm understanding of adult learning theory and infuse their sessions with opportunities for the learners to feel that they have some choice and that the learning is immediately relevant to them.

Corporate trainers may be evaluated with similar KPIs to

instructional designers – number of sessions delivered, employee engagement and satisfaction, etc. The most relevant KPIs for business leaders, though, are again the ones that relate to ROI. High Net Promoter Scores, increase in organizational performance metrics, decrease in errors on the job, and other measures of job skill improvements will be key measures of performance.

The median pay in 2020 for trainers was $62,700. The market for trainers is steadily increasing, with a 9% forecasted growth rate between now and 2029.[38] After about five years of experience, many trainers are able to advance to a training and development manager role, with a median salary of $115,640.[39]

*****

ACCOUNT EXECUTIVE/SALES

One of the most common things I hear teachers say is, "I don't want to do sales." I can't say I blame them. In the past, I always said that too. As a matter of fact, in my coaching and consultant work, I often made a point to tell my clients that I was not involved in the sale of the product at all in a misguided attempt to appear more trustworthy to the teacher. I wanted them to correctly infer that I was not being paid a commission based on whether they used the product.

However, as you have likely picked up on by now, most careers in a company in some way involve sales. Everyone who works for a company is expected to speak well of the products and services they offer and promote additional products and services. It's only natural. We have probably all had a laugh at the irony of seeing someone wearing a uniform from one fast-food restaurant picking up their lunch from a competitor down the street, or a grocery store employee shopping at another store. It doesn't look good for their own company. In the same way, *every* employee for a company – whether in a specific sales role or not – has the responsibility to promote the company's products and services.

Teachers should be willing to consider a sales position. Many teachers will likely find that sales is a great fit and also allows them greater financial freedom and control over their financial goals. One sales executive I spoke with said, "People join sales because they want to make money while being able to help people." Sales positions can also be about helping others. When you truly believe something is good for students and teachers, you want to tell others about it. Why not make your passion for a product something that provides your income?

However, not *all* teachers will be successful in this role. Some teachers may never be able to overcome their inhibitions about sales. Therefore, it is important to understand what traits contribute to being a successful sales representative and to closely evaluate your own skills in this area before applying to such a position.

The sales team is the lifeblood of any EdTech company. Without adding new customers, a company cannot grow, and without growth, a company likely will not survive. One study revealed that companies with higher annual revenues had fewer and fewer competitors because it is so difficult for a company to *keep* growing over time. Very few companies survive to the point where they become an educational behemoth.[40]

In the education world, adding new customers is no easy task. The K–12 market in specific is very decentralized.[41] Individual schools, teams within the schools, or even lone teachers often make their own decisions about the platforms they use, which can make it incredibly difficult for a sales representative (otherwise known as an account executive, account manager, or territory manager) to get an "enterprise sale" – a large sale involving an entire district or network of schools. As teachers well know, it is often very difficult to get to the right people to have a sale approved in education. There is generally a long process involving multiple people and multiple votes, and after lots of hard work on the part of the account manager, there are often more nos than yeses when it comes to making that final sale.

If you are passionate about sharing the benefits of a product you love with others, you *might* be a good candidate for a sales position. But passion alone does not make for greatness. So what are some of the key traits of high-performing account executives? Many of these qualities are summarized in the research study cited above from Fuel, a McKinsey Company.

Let's start with what is *not* necessarily the best quality – and that is, surprisingly, empathy. Although it may be helpful to have a background as a teacher, being *too* empathetic might make it more difficult for you to push to close a sale or walk away instead of offering discounts or freebies. Empathizing more with a school's budget cuts than with your own company's need to keep increasing revenue will mean that you do a disservice to your employer. A certain amount of empathy might help – being able to say that you know what it is like as a teacher or administrator – but a company cannot survive by constantly giving away their product. They *must* make money to survive. Put another way, the company must make money to pay your salary and the salary of all your colleagues. School budgets are created from money provided by the government (aside from private schools, of course, which rely on tuition, and charter schools which supplement government funding with business partnerships in many cases). But your corporate employer is funded by the schools that purchase their products. Without those customers, the company dies. As an account executive, you *must* empathize more with your company's needs than your client's.

So what *are* some of the key traits needed? Certainly diligence. Sales reps cannot give up, even when 90% of the clients they pursue say no. It helps for them to be detail oriented as they work tirelessly to close multiple deals across large territories. They need to be energetic and people-oriented as well as excellent communicators – listening for the hidden and often unexpressed needs of potential customers. Sales reps are also excellent at identifying leads, which involves research. They need to find potential customers, evaluate what their needs might be, determine how much value the potential customer might bring to the company, and then initiate conversations with the potential to drive them toward a deal, in some cases before the customer even begins a conversation with the company.

Good sales reps are often motivated by financial rewards. In many EdTech companies, the base salaries of account executives are generally lower than one might expect. They are paid an additional commission based on the revenue they generate for the company. Good sales reps love the chase. They love knowing that if they close this deal, there will be a reward for them. And that reward can be significant.

If you find yourself faltering at this, then a sales role will likely not be a good fit for you. Stick with one of the other positions discussed in this chapter. But if this excites you and sounds like something you would do well, you might want to consider some entry-level sales positions. These positions might be titled Business Development Representative, Sales Development Representative or Inbound Sales Representative. These positions generally work more with inbound sales – sales that are made when a customer reaches out and expresses interest in the product first. Other more entry-level positions involve outbound sales – sales generated when a sales rep initiates the conversation with a potential customer. These positions are sometimes titled Account Manager or Account Associate. However, since companies often use different terms for their sales team members, it is most important to evaluate the job description. Generally, if the position requires 3+ years of experience, it is *not* an entry-level position.

It is likely obvious that the KPIs for an account manager will relate to the number of deals they close and the total revenue they bring into the company. Companies may look at how often the account manager or executive reached out to clients, how many meetings they held, and how many contacts were made, but what matters most is, did all that hard work have a return on investment?

Salaries for EdTech and educational publishing account managers and executives vary greatly. The difference has to do with how much companies offer as a base salary and how they formulate the added commissions. This variability in base salaries is also notable from one source to the next. According to Glassdoor®, the average base salary for educational sales representatives is around $48,500. However, this does not include commissions earned. You could make up to about $70,000 with commission included. As you gain experience in sales and move from entry-level sales positions into mid- and higher-level positions, the base salary increases to up to as much as about $75,000.[42] Again, these ranges will vary based on the company. "The Education & Technology Sales Compensation and Industry Status Report 2020" published by The Renaissance Network (TRN) includes a breakdown of the average salaries by age range, with the lowest average base salary for an educational sales representative reported for those between the ages of 25 and 34 years old and listed as $76,050. Notably, though, fewer than 5% of TRN's respondents had been on the job for less than two years.[43] Companies with larger base salaries likely will provide less variable compensation, including commission.

*****

SUMMARY

There are numerous roles teachers considering a career change can consider when pondering a transition to EdTech. With so many options, how do you decide which ones to apply for? Which ones are you most likely to be considered for?

One recruiter I spoke to shared that any position that requires 3+ years of experience in a similar role would not be considered an entry-level position. And remember, no matter how many years of classroom experience you have, because you are transitioning to a new field, you will most likely be considered entry level. Therefore, after considering the roles described above and deciding which ones you are open to, read job descriptions carefully and look for those that do not require several years of experience. In general, avoid anything with "senior" in the title.

*****

REFLECTION QUESTIONS

1. Am I comfortable having conversations with customers about aspects of sales such as invoices that have come due or other products or services they should consider purchasing? (If not, do not pursue sales or customer success positions.)
2. What aspects of each position excite me? What aspects would be more difficult?

3. What salary range am I comfortable with, and does that range work for an entry-level position in the role I am exploring?
4. Am I OK with working on a base salary with some of my pay being based on commission?
5. Now that I have an idea of what roles I am most interested in, what can I do to make myself stand out to recruiters? (Not sure? More on that in the next chapter.)

5

WHAT CAN I DO TO INCREASE MY CHANCES OF GETTING A JOB?

"I am in the journey of transitioning [out of] education. I have been applying to jobs for the past few months with limited luck. What tips does anyone have for changing careers?"

-Teacher post, LinkedIn®, 2021

*****

Landing a job in EdTech is not easy. I spoke with a human resources manager recently who told me that for one small company of fewer than 50 employees, she receives approximately 800 applications per week for advertised positions. There is a *lot* of competition. The competition comes not only from teachers like you who are pursuing a career change, but also from countless others already in the corporate world who have either been laid off (especially during Covid) or those who are currently working and looking to change positions.

I have seen numerous teachers post that they are quitting the classroom to pursue a job in EdTech. What concerns me about this is that there seems to be a false narrative that any teacher can quickly get a job working for an EdTech company. That is not the case. Often it takes months to get a job, or even an interview. Many teachers who apply to positions will find themselves back in the classroom the following year, frustrated in a process that they didn't understand or that they believe failed them. Some publicly share their frustration, commenting on social media that companies should "give them a chance."

So, how does one break into the corporate world of education? How does one "get the chance"? There is no magical formula, sadly, but there are some practical tips to consider. In this chapter, I will break down these tips one at a time. Hopefully, by implementing these ideas, you will find yourself in the role you are seeking!

*****

TIP #1: LEARN MORE ABOUT EDUCATION

First of all, by "learn" I do *not* mean, "Go get another master's degree." In many cases, you do *not* need to pursue another degree unless you wish to pursue a career within education itself. If you decided after reading the first few chapters of this book to stay within the field of education, then pursuing a degree in educational leadership, adult learning or some other field might be beneficial for you. Higher positions in education often do require advanced degrees. However, in the corporate world, as mentioned in the last chapter, a degree is not always needed. Experience is often more important. So, don't immediately go sign up for another degree unless you really want it and see a practical need for it.

What I mean by "learn" is, do everything you can to learn about the current educational system – both within education and within the corporate world. There are many areas to explore that can help you advance your career. For example, if you are currently in a school setting, consider asking if you can learn how purchasing works. What is a PO, and how is that different from an invoice? What is the budgeting cycle for the school year? How does budgeting work in your school, and who makes the decisions? Ask your principal or business manager how often they interact with educational vendors, and what that process is like. Which vendors do they really appreciate, and why? Which ones do they avoid, and why do they avoid them?

Have you attended your school board meetings? If not, do! Learn how local districts make decisions. Learn about consent agendas and what gets put on them. How are school district committees set up, and who serves on them? How are those individuals selected? Get to know your board members. Network within your district. Sometimes, as in my case, it is these connections that can help you get a foot in the door at an educational company.

Consider spending some time and research on learning about educational policies for your school, district, or state. How are these policies created? What is the process? How do educational lobbyists and teachers' unions factor in? How can policies be changed?

Learning about the current educational process can help you both within the field of education itself and in your future role with an education company. If you have inside knowledge as to how educational leaders think and make decisions, it will help you when you need to interact with those leaders as a customer success manager, consultant, or account manager. Many companies are looking for people experienced with speaking to educational leaders – principals, assistant superintendents, and superintendents. Educational leaders talk differently about education. They must view the big picture, synthesize data from various sources without getting too in the weeds, and make decisions that will impact hundreds or thousands of teachers and students. Learning *how* they do this will help you as you work alongside them in the future. The best time to learn that is while you are still an insider working with them in the school district.

*****

TIP #2: LEARN MORE ABOUT THE ROLE

The corporate world is *very* different from the educational world. There are parallels, of course, but there are a lot of differences. Your teaching experience is valuable, but you need to ensure that you can speak to the role you are pursuing. If you are a teacher seeking a position as a customer success manager, for example, you need to ensure that you "speak CSM," or if you want to be a corporate trainer, that you can speak to "adult learning theory." Too many teachers think that their skills are immediately transferable. Many skills are, but with hundreds of applications for each position, if you want to stand out you need to show that you understand the job!

The first way to learn about a job is to ask lots of questions about it. If you do not already have a LinkedIn® professional networking services profile, create one right away, and start using it to connect with people who have the role you are looking for. You can then join various groups dedicated to specific areas of interest. For example, one group known as the Customer Success Forum currently has over 44,000 members, while a group dedicated to instructional design has over 23,000 members. Join these groups, and then start learning from them.

As you look for a job in a specific area, ask people who have that job to describe their day to you. What does the day in the life of a customer success manager look like? Or an instructional designer? Or a corporate trainer? What do they love about their jobs? What makes their job different from teaching? Ask, ask, ask! Find out all you can about each type of position. The information will help you identify other personal growth opportunities and also speak to the role during your interview. *When you are interviewing, you must know what the job entails!* If you have no idea what the job would involve, the interview will result in you still searching. (In my own recent experience job hunting, I was asked in every interview what I thought the position involved. You never want to say, "I don't really know." You need to have at least a general idea of what the job does and why you would be a good fit for it!)

How do you find people to ask? You can certainly ask to connect with or send InMail® messages to people on LinkedIn® whom you have never met before and who currently are in a role similar to the one you are seeking. You might find these people randomly, but you can also search for people with the job title you desire using the search feature. When you find someone with the role you are interested in, you can view their recent activity. This is helpful because you want to know if they actually might see your request to connect or your message. (Many people have LinkedIn® accounts, but not everyone is on there often.) If you *do* ask to connect with someone you don't have any real-life connection to, make sure to introduce yourself and explain why you want to connect. Many people don't respond to requests to connect or vague messages that just say, "I'd like to connect." Explain why you want to connect. They may not reply, but you certainly haven't lost anything by asking!

A better strategy might be to search for connections you already have with that title. The search feature on LinkedIn®

allows you to enter a job title and search for that title among people. From there, you can filter by your first, second, and third connections. If you have any "1ˢᵗ" connections with that title, reach out to them first for advice. You may not, though. In that case, a great second step is to search for your 2ⁿᵈ connections. These are people who are connected with someone that you also know. When you view your 2ⁿᵈ connections, you can click on their name to view their "mutual connections." These are the people you both know on this platform. From there, you could ask one of those individuals to introduce you. I have had this happen several times over the past year. Someone reached out to me to say, "I have a friend trying to break into EdTech. Would you mind connecting with them and sharing your thoughts?" When I received those messages, I always said yes.

If you have no first or second connections in a job like one you are seeking, don't worry! LinkedIn® also has many professional groups that you can join to connect with people. For example, a search for Customer Success Manager in Groups leads to many groups from all over the world that you can join to ask questions or share ideas.

Once you have decided to pursue a certain role, take free classes online to build foundational knowledge or brush up on skills. I have used LinkedIn Learning® courses quite a bit, as they have certifications that you can then post on your profile page once you complete them. (LinkedIn Learning® is not free and does require a monthly subscription, but their content is excellent.) However, there are many different sites that offer online courses – from Coursera® to Khan Academy®. Consider looking up courses that have to do with the role itself. For example, search for courses using keywords such as "fundamentals of customer success management" or "basics of adult learning theory" or "instructional design for beginners." I found it helpful to take several different courses about the same field as each one reinforces the new knowledge and offers a different perspective.

As you learn from these courses, take notes. What questions do they cause you to ask? For example, if the introductory course mentions the ADDIE model and you don't immediately know what they are talking about, that is your next step for learning. Jot the idea down, and when you finish the course, take another in ADDIE. Many of the courses on LinkedIn® are part of a series made up of several modules. If you look up "What is ADDIE?" you might find that it is module 4 of a 16-module course. In that case, I recommend completing the entire course.

Another way to prepare for a specific role is to examine multiple job postings for that type of position. What do the postings have in common? For example, EdTech customer success management positions currently use acronyms like SaaS, CRM, or ROI. Do you know what those terms mean? If not, it's OK! Just do a quick search and learn what they mean.

As you analyze job postings, also look for common platform or software proficiency requirements. Current instructional design positions, for example, often list Adobe Creative Suite, Articulate 360, and Captivate as prerequisite proficiencies, as well as LMS experience. You do not need to take college courses to become proficient in a software program! Rather, when you find an area in which you lack proficiency, search for online courses or tutorials on YouTube®. Become a Google® certified teacher, take courses on Microsoft® Suite, and look at the Help section of platform websites, where learning videos and articles are often embedded. Play around with free versions of software available to you. (Even some customer relationship management systems, or CRMs, have free versions that you can try out for an unlimited amount of time.) Pick an area that you know will add value to your resume and focus on that. Don't become a jack of all trades and master of none. Choose something and learn it well. Then utilize it in your current position to make the learning stick, especially if you haven't landed your ideal job yet. To ensure that you are not overwhelmed while still teaching, focus on platforms that will bring you value in the classroom as well as in the corporate world. For example, if your school or district currently uses Canvas® as your LMS, don't try to become an expert in PowerSchool®. Look up the Help articles and tutorials for the platforms you currently use in your district. Master those. That will help you both in your classroom and in your search. Learning an instructional design software program? Try creating a lesson for an upcoming unit of study in your classroom or a training you are going to share with colleagues.

*****

TIP #3: USE WHAT YOU LEARN TO GAIN EXPERIENCE AS A LEADER

One recruiter I spoke with shared with me that too many teachers talk only about their classroom work on resumes or interviews. They talk about working in a racially and economically diverse classroom, using different teaching practices for engagement or reading instruction, or how they created diverse lesson plans. In the corporate world, these do not need to be listed on a resume. What the corporate world wants to know is, how do you work with *adults?* You need to show your experience interacting with *and leading* adults to really stand out. Being a leader is not synonymous with managing others. Look for opportunities right now to put your learning into practice by serving as a team leader or on a committee or task force, or by facilitating a workshop to share your learning with others. This will not only give you practical experience but will also help you stand out from others by showing that you have moved beyond the basic role of a teacher.

Consider how you can use your learning experiences and transfer your skills to a new position. Are you applying for a customer success or implementation position? When in your teaching experience did you help your school or district onboard with a new system, curriculum, or program? Did you help train other teachers? Did you help with rostering or scheduling? Did you become the "mentor" teacher for a particular platform? Or, if you are applying for an instructional designer or corporate trainer role, when did you design learning for your colleagues? How did you know what skills they needed? What type of training did you deliver, and how did you measure success? How about a sales position? If you served on a fundraising or business partnership committee, how did you determine the funds that were needed? How did you pursue partners and meet or exceed your goal? Learn *and highlight* how you work with adults on your resume, not how well you worked with children.

The main question to keep asking is "How can I use this new knowledge to benefit the *adults* around me as well?" For example, most schools use an LMS and it is likely that not everyone in your school or district has the same level of proficiency. If you learn some great tips for the LMS you currently use, can you design an online course or in-person, after-school PD session to share with your colleagues? Keep building and tracking those *adult* interactions, and the value that those interactions add to your school. If you can set goals around this, that's even better. For example, if your goal is to train the entire 4th grade team (maybe 15% of a school's teaching staff) on how to effectively use Google Classroom®, but it goes so well that you are then asked to train the entire staff, share that! You exceeded your goal! And then, what was the result? Follow up with teachers later to see how many still use it. Don't forget parents as well! If you don't have the opportunity to train *teachers* this year, is there a way you can bring value to *parents*? Can you design a short training to show them how and why to do repeated one-minute timed readings, how to navigate a school's website, or how to find the parent support section on a curriculum website? If so, follow up with a Google Forms® survey to ask for feedback and use this survey information to make your sessions even more effective.

Ultimately, you want to build your resume to show that you are not just a great teacher for *children*, but that you can also add value to your organization because of the work you do with *adults*.

*****

TIP #4: POLISH YOUR SOCIAL MEDIA PROFILES

If you do not have a LinkedIn® profile, stop reading and go create one. Seriously. And while you're at it, be sure to create an account on Indeed® too. Come back when you have that done!

Indeed® and LinkedIn® are the top job aggregators used by recruiters.[44] For many corporate positions today, applications can be submitted directly from these sites, and many positions request your LinkedIn® profile even if you are not applying via LinkedIn®. So what is the difference between them and how should you use them?

Indeed® does not have the social networking features that LinkedIn® does, but it is the number one search engine for job listings in the world.[45] You want to have your resume ready to go and have a profile created on Indeed® so that you can easily apply for jobs when they appear there.

LinkedIn® allows you to showcase your work and expertise, using your own words as well as written recommendations from others. (Did you get some great feedback from a colleague on a training you led? You can send them a message using InMail® to ask them to write you a recommendation right there on LinkedIn® and display it on your profile.) It allows you to highlight your best work and your certifications.

And of course, LinkedIn® allows you to network. In some cases, employees who wish to refer friends or acquaintances for open positions in their company simply send the link from their recruiter directly to the individual's LinkedIn® account, or vice versa. In one company I have worked for, I could send my connection's LinkedIn® profile link directly to my company's recruiter, referring someone for a position even before they applied!

One note on networking, though. LinkedIn® is a fantastic place to connect with people at different organizations, but you want to consider that many on LinkedIn® don't just connect with everyone who sends them a connection request. In general, connect with those you truly do know in person, and choose to *follow* those you do not know personally. If you really want to connect with someone you have not met before, be sure to add a note to your connection request. Asking to connect with no note attached can be viewed as presumptuous.

Since recruiters often use LinkedIn® to research you before an interview, you want to make sure that your profile is top-notch. Always include a professional-looking headshot and information on how to contact you. Use the tips LinkedIn® provides to make your profile stronger, including changing your banner, adding a strong headline, and writing an excellent summary. (LinkedIn Learning® offers courses to help you learn the platform and use it to really market yourself.) Then return on a regular basis to update your profile with new information. And be sure to review all of your settings to decide your profile's visibility, your communication preferences, and how you want to let recruiters know of your interest.

*****

TIP #5: START WITH COMPANIES YOU KNOW

As a teacher, you already have experience with certain products. Think of the publishers whose curriculum you have been using for years. There are LMSs, platforms and software your school or district uses. Make a list of all of these. Think of the ones you particularly loved or got to know well – the ones you championed, even if they weren't perfect. These are the places to start.

Companies want teachers who can speak authentically to their own experiences with their products and services. When you are a professional consultant who is training or coaching 30 teachers, your in-depth knowledge of the curriculum and what it offers is incredibly valuable. When you are working as an implementation manager and supporting a school with analyzing data from your company's platform, your experience is beneficial. A company bringing on a former teacher with experience in their products or services will have a faster return on investment because they may not need to spend as much time on training. In addition, your experience with the platform will give you confidence as you transition to a new industry.

So, start here. Follow these companies online. Sign up for notifications on their careers page. Highlight on your LinkedIn® profile your familiarity and daily use of their products. Post or comment on their company-run social media pages. If you post often, they notice! You become a digital advocate and they see you. (Sometimes EdTech companies will look for teachers to test out their platform. If you see this, sign up! It's a great way to get some experience with the product, and there is often an incentive involved.) And, if they offer a conference or teacher certification process of some sort, sign up for it and complete it!

A note of caution, though. When you do land an interview with one of these companies, do not try to come across as an expert. Companies benefit from people familiar with their products, but it can be detrimental to hire someone who thinks they know everything about the product and wants to be viewed as an expert right away. It is better to enter the position from the standpoint of a learner with some experience. You may accidentally turn people off if you present yourself as an expert.

*****

TIP #6: GET TO KNOW OTHER COMPANIES

Although starting with companies you know is a good first step, certainly explore other companies as well. Create job alerts on LinkedIn® and Indeed® for jobs from specific companies or with specific titles. When those jobs appear, begin to research the companies that interest you.

Companies want to know that the individuals they are hiring are truly interested in them. As you prepare for an interview, or post on social media about a company to try to capture their attention, consider learning more about them. What is their mission? Does their mission excite you and can you share that with others? What is their niche market? (This is incredibly helpful to know because it may help you stand out. For example, if you are applying for a position with an educational publishing company that focuses on early childhood education through grade 12, and you have experience with preschool education, you can highlight how your experience would benefit their pre-K outreach. Or, if you are applying as a content writer, it is helpful to know if the content you will be writing will be aimed at the K–3 market or higher education!)

Do a general search for the company online. After reviewing the company's website, look to see what others are saying about them. Is the press generally good? You may find that a company just went through four rounds of layoffs which should cause some alarm bells to go off in your mind. You may also discover tidbits that can help you stand out, like that the company has plans to expand its offerings into Latin America. If you speak fluent Spanish, that would be an excellent skill to highlight during an interview, even mentioning that you have read about their expansion goals.

Next, do an online search for "employee morale" at the company you are interviewing with. Indeed® and other websites often shares ratings by current employees of morale within that organization, and this can be very valuable to your decision making. If a company is described over and over as being toxic or demoralizing by more than a handful of people, that is something to pay attention to. On the other hand, you may learn that in general people respect the leadership, define the culture as amazing, and value the overall mission of the company. This can help you with formulating your answer to the common interview question, "Why do you want to work for us?"

Research their platforms, products, and services as well. If an EdTech company you are interested in working for offers a free account, sign up! You don't have to use the platform with your students, but if you can, that's great. However, do try out their features yourself at least. One common question you will be asked in an interview is whether you have tested out their platform. You are *not* expected to be an expert in the platform, but you most definitely should be able to speak to its basic functionality. Be prepared to share that you created an account and tried out a few things and share what you enjoyed about the experience.

Another common question I was asked during interviews was, "What suggestions for improvement or questions about [the product] do you have?" This question is a great way for interviewers to gauge whether or not you really *did* spend time with their product. So, as you tinker with a free account on a platform, take notes. What features do you like? What do you wonder? What might be helpful that the company may not have considered?

A second note of caution here: when you are interviewing, don't try to pretend that you tried out a platform if you didn't really. The interviewer likely can do a quick search to see that you have not actually created an account. If you created the account under an alias or with a different email address than you used to apply for the position, mention that. (Better yet, use the same email and your real name.)

Learn who the company's competitors are as well. Sometimes interviewers ask what you know about the company. Mentioning some of their competitors will show that you have done your research. A quick online search will reveal this information, and you may find that you have direct experience with a competitor's products in your classroom. This experience may also be of value to a company. If hired, you may be able to share insights about how the competitor's product compares to ones offered by the company at which you are interviewing, for example. Although EdTech companies do not generally speak directly with customers about their competitors for ethical reasons, it would certainly be valuable to a company to know that a competitor offers a favorite feature that their product does not offer, for example.

How might this help you during an interview? I certainly do not recommend saying something to the effect of, "I can tell you exactly how your competitor's products work." Instead, you can fit it into the conversation when the company asks what you know about their product and what questions you might have. Asking something to the effect of, "As I was testing out this program, I wondered about ___. As a teacher, we used [competitor company's product] in my school, which I know is one of your competitors. I always found that I wished they had [some great feature that this company's product offers.] Your product does this, which I was so excited about! I did wonder, though, if your product also includes [something the competitor's product does.]" Asking a question like this shows that you have really gone above and beyond to think about not just the product, but also the company and their competition.

Another great way to research companies is to attend EdTech conferences. There are numerous EdTech conferences that occur virtually and in person throughout the world each year. Search for conferences done by Future of Education Technology (FETC), International Society for Technology in Education (ISTE), or Computer-Using Educators (CUE). These conferences are a great opportunity to learn more about the industry and different EdTech companies while also networking with others.

*****

TIP #7: START SMALL

Occasionally on social media sites, I see career coaches marketing their services by stating that they will help teachers land that dream six-figure job in EdTech. They may very well be able to do that. However, I would encourage you to temper your salary expectations somewhat to make as you transition into the EdTech world from the classroom. Six figures may be possible with time, but it is definitely not the norm right away.

It is important to have a goal in mind for what you would like your salary to be. However, it is also important to be realistic about what you will be able to do right away. Some of the best advice a recruiter shared with me is to be willing to start small. There are two different ways to consider this. She meant that teachers need to understand that by switching careers, they are essentially starting over. Their experience in the classroom is valuable, but they are brand new to a new industry and therefore need to be willing to compromise.

What does this compromise look like for you? Essentially, you need to be willing to accept what are considered entry-level positions in the corporate world. Your five years of classroom experience do not equal five years of corporate experience. You may need to take a lower salary than you anticipated or settle for different benefits than your ideal position or start in a slightly different role. It will help you to adjust to the corporate world if you recognize this and are willing to "start small" – as if you are beginning your career. You have a lot more experience and knowledge than you once had, and you will likely be given the opportunity to grow into other positions with higher salaries if you desire, but you may not land that ideal job right away.

On the other hand, starting small could mean starting with contract, per diem, or part-time work. This was my experience. This type of work is easier to find for some roles than for others. For example, it might be easier to find work as a contract content writer than as a professional consultant. Consider applying for those part time jobs. They may be your foot in the door.

In some cases, a company may be seeking someone to do contract work during evenings or weekends. In this case, continuing to work as a teacher while picking up a "side hustle" would be an option to consider. I know of one company that hires veteran teachers to coach other teachers online after school, for example. Another company hires teachers to write its assessments and online courses.

Of course, working two different jobs is not possible for many people. However, teachers who have already left the classroom but who have yet to get the offer for a full-time position should not ignore part-time options. Many companies today offer part-time positions more frequently than they do full-time roles. The difficulty for employees is that these roles often do not come with insurance. However, they can pay very well! In one of my past roles, I was hired as a "per diem" consultant. This meant that I could work just a few days a week if I wanted to. Within a short time, I was working a full-time schedule even though I was officially "per diem." Although I didn't have health insurance benefits, I made more money per day than I did as a full-time employee. With this additional income, I purchased health insurance separately. Eventually, this led to a full-time position in the company, with benefits.

Part-time positions can be a great way to introduce yourself to a company, learn valuable skills and experiences, and ultimately find the full-time position you desire. If you haven't had any luck landing a full-time position, consider part-time work.

Additionally, you may even want to consider offering to intern at an EdTech company during the summers. Smaller startup companies might be more willing to do this and would likely be more interested if they know that you bring experience with their platform in the classroom. Although the position may not pay a lot, the experience might lead to a regular job.

*****

TIP #8: DON'T BE AFRAID TO REACH OUT

When I was searching for a job, I spent hours every day looking at the job postings and applying for advertised positions. I knew that I should network, and I did that to the best of my ability as well. The most helpful advice I received, though, came in the form of a LinkedIn Learning® course about seeking a new job. In this course called "Find a Job in the Hidden Job Market," Sarah Johnston, the instructor and a career coach, shared something that I suspected but had never quite known for sure: *many jobs never even get posted.*

This isn't nepotism or favoritism. This is called the "hidden job market." This is simply the result of a company discovering someone who would benefit their company and offering or *creating* a position for them. Someone refers a person they know or introduces them to a CEO or director, and after connecting, a position is offered to the referred individual. Johnston states that up to 70% of people find their next job through a referral by someone in their network.

This means that you should not be afraid to network – especially asking for help among those professional relationships you already have! If you are able, share your career goals with your colleagues and leadership to see if they can help you meet others who might be able to help you.

What if you don't know anyone who can help you? First, use LinkedIn®'s network to see if you know anyone who has a connection with someone at the company. By looking at your connections' networks, you can often find someone else who might be able to introduce you. For example, maybe a colleague or friend happens to be connected to the business manager of a new startup. Your friend might be willing to forward your resume to that person and introduce you.

I do not advise asking someone you don't know at all to refer you. In that case my advice would be to reach out directly to the hiring manager or recruiter. Why should someone you don't know introduce you to someone else you don't know? Just introduce yourself!

Consider looking at the company's team page and look for their human resources person or a director in the area in which you would like to work. Send them a message and tell them your history and interest in their products or services. Ask if they might be willing to connect by phone or meet with you virtually or in person. This would be a good chance to show how your skills can help them overcome any challenges they may be experiencing or market gaps that came up in your research of the company. Share your excitement. Be professional, upbeat, and positive.

Does that work? Not always, of course, but *yes!* I have personally experienced success with this. I have also seen others experience a degree of success with this method. It may work better with smaller companies, but by reaching out, you are introducing yourself, and you have the opportunity to suggest areas in which you could help that the company may not have considered.

What if you apply for a position and never hear back, even if you still see the position posted online? Does that mean it was a definite *no*? Not necessarily. Sometimes the advertised position has been put on hold for a period and hiring hasn't occurred yet. If you applied for a position and don't hear back, and if it is a position you are really interested in, you have nothing to lose by reaching out to ask about it. When you do, consider sending your resume again, attached to the message, to allow the recipient to glance at it quickly. I have received valuable information by following up to ask about a position, and actually got my most recent position by doing this as well. Just don't do this too soon. In general, I would wait a few weeks before inquiring.

What if you interview for a position and then don't hear anything back? Is it rude to reach out again? This can vary from one recruiter to another, of course, but the advice I have been given most often is that it is fine to reach out – especially if the interviewer told you that you would hear back after a certain amount of time and that time has passed. Remember that recruiters and managers are busy people as well. They are not intentionally rude. They may be interviewing hundreds of people for different positions, and they just don't always remember to follow up. Sending them a gentle nudge is acceptable. Consider politely reminding them of your interview, stating that you are still very interested in the position, and asking if they might know when you will hear of any next steps. Don't assume that their silence equates to disinterest in hiring you. It may be that right in the middle of hiring, the company had to put the position on hold for a few weeks. (This happens more often than you might think.) The recruiter may just not have had the time to inform everyone.

And if you do get that rejection letter, then what? I always replied to the sender and thanked them for letting me know. I also asked if they have any feedback on the interview that I might be able to learn from. Usually I received no response, which I have been told could be due to legal concerns. On occasion, though, I would get a reply with incredible insight and advice to help me know just where I did not meet the expectations, and I used that advice to improve my job or interview skills the next time. If they are kind enough to send you that feedback, thank them for that!

*****

TIP #9: TAILOR YOUR RESUME

The absolute best advice given to me during my job search was shared by Wes Brach, founder of Ideal Resume™. I got to know Wes when a friend who knew I was job-searching connected us on LinkedIn®. Wes was starting his platform, idealresume.com, and was looking for individuals to test it out. Wes gave me the best resume advice I received during my job hunt. What was so stunning to me was how contradictory it was to almost everything I thought I knew about writing a good resume.

I had what I thought was a great resume. I had summarized all my previous work using strong verbs and buzzwords. I had created a PDF with stellar graphics, two columns, and my contact information summarized neatly with icons to show how to reach me by phone, email, or LinkedIn®. It looked like images of stellar resumes I found online but personalized by and for me. It looked great!

Wes asked me to send him my resume and set up a call with me to review it. I'll be honest—I was a complete skeptic. I only met with him because after two months of searching, I hadn't found any work, and I was getting desperate.

The first thing Wes told me was a complete shock. He said, "Get rid of all the graphics. Get rid of the columns and the icons. Go back to using a Word® document and don't put anything fancy in it. Then save it as a Word® document and upload it to job sites as such."

Wes explained to me that my original resume would be great, if we lived at a time when I was hand-delivering my resume at a job fair and I was sure that it was getting into the hands of an actual human. But we don't. We live in an age where an applicant tracking system (otherwise known as an ATS) is used by a company to sift through hundreds of resumes, finding only the best ones to pass along for review by a human.

Applicant tracking systems are used by almost all companies that accept online applications for job postings. With hundreds of applications for *each* job being submitted, the ATS quickly analyzes each resume and compares it to the original text of the job description, looking for the best matches. The ATS looks for keywords and skills and flags the resumes with the highest match for the human recruiter to review. All others go unseen by the human! As a matter of fact, according to Ideal Resume, up to 70% of resumes are rejected by the ATS, never to be seen by the human recruiter.

There are some key things to understand about an ATS. First of all, an ATS does not always understand subtle differences between words and certainly will not be able to draw inferences like a human. For example, do not assume that the ATS will understand that your history of delivering "online webinars and virtual classes" means the same thing as the job description, which is looking for someone who can "facilitate synchronous and asynchronous e-Learning courses." If the words don't match, the ATS often does not draw the conclusion that a human would. Even using synonyms can cause you to be rejected. If the job description says "facilitate professional learning" and your resume says "lead professional development," you will not be a match!

Secondly, the ATS doesn't know what to do with graphics and columns. ATSs are designed to read from left to right. If you have a two-column resume, the ATS will often combine the first line in the first column with the first line in the second column, making your resume complete gibberish. And if you put a graphic somewhere, it can completely throw off the ATS. Hence, Wes's advice to go back to a simple resume format. Additionally, ATSs work best with Microsoft Word® documents. Unless a job description specifically requests that you send a PDF, send your resume as a Word doc. (Have you ever uploaded your resume when applying for a job and then found that you had to re-enter all your information in numerous fields because it was either missing or convoluted? Welcome to the ATS trying to autofill the fields for you and running into some difficulty.)

Wes's information was a game-changer for me. I used his resume analyzer on the Ideal Resume site in which I would quickly copy and paste a company's job description on one side and my resume on the other. The analyzer would compare the two and tell me my match score. (ATSs look for at least an 80% match.) It would also give me tips on how to increase my score – what skills were needed, for example, and even link me to courses where I could learn those skills. Sometimes I would make basic tweaks to my resume. For example, I often noticed that my score went up when I listed the full suite of programs offered by Microsoft® instead of just listing "Microsoft Suite" if a job description listed them all. Other times I realized that the ATS was looking for "Software as a Service," but I had listed "SaaS," or vice versa. This quick tool helped me make tweaks to my resume for each job I applied for.

We did discover one notable "bug" with ATSs, though. No matter what I did to my resume, my match score often came up lacking. For some reason, my carefully crafted EdTech resume always was read by an ATS as being a better fit for human resources or clerical work. It didn't seem to be a problem with Wes's site. My husband tested it out using his resume and career field and the site worked perfectly well for him, with quick tweaks to his resume getting him above that 80% score. I contacted Wes, and he and I met again. Wes was completely perplexed and decided to ask his contacts at ATS companies. Although every ATS company is slightly different, the ATS companies reported at the time that there was a known issue with tracking resumes geared toward EdTech and educational publishing (and at the time of this book's publishing, Wes confirmed that it still seemed to be an issue). This means that even if your resume matches perfectly, it may still not be flagged as a good fit.

This was incredibly helpful to know. Once I discovered this, I began following up personally on jobs I desired if some time had gone by and I hadn't heard back from the company. I emailed a few human resource managers, attached my "beautiful PDF copy" of my resume, and shared with them that I had discovered that ATS platforms have an issue reading my resume and matching it to their job description. I almost always got a reply message from the contact.

That being said, if there is a position that you truly believe you have all the qualifications for and you haven't heard back, it could be that it has to do with the ATS. Don't assume you aren't a good fit. Find another professional way to reach out, introduce yourself, share your passion and desire to work for the company and why, and ask them to consider reviewing your attached resume.

One additional note: I came to rely so much on Ideal Resume that I continue to work with Wes. Ideal Resume is the one company in this book that I now have an affiliation with. If you are interested in learning more about this tool and using it for yourself, you can do so on my affiliate site at https://idealresume.idevaffiliate.com/106.html.

*****

TIP #10: PRESENT YOUR MOST PROFESSIONAL SELF

I was working with a group of teachers all trying to move into the EdTech world several months ago. They shared some of their struggles with me as they tried to navigate this transition. From their comments come the following tips, which I summarize under the heading to *present your most professional self.*

First and foremost, do not assume you have nothing to offer. Have you been working with preschoolers? Your input is valuable to EdTech and educational publishing companies that are creating content for young learners. You know them better than anyone else! Remember that companies have a niche market (early childhood, K–12, elementary, secondary, higher education, STEM, etc.). Find the companies that match the niche you belong to and focus on them.

I was once asked if it would be wise to share a digital portfolio with a potential employer. My answer was, not unless they ask. In my experience, the digital content or presentations created by teachers, no matter how impressive, are not usually up to the standards of an organization with very specific ideas around how to market their brand. You don't want to accidentally eliminate yourself because you used a font that the company detests or because you didn't align everything in your PowerPoint the right way. Teachers create content quickly for use with students for a day or two – and though the content may be good, it is not going to be the same caliber as content created by a marketing team or those with training in specific presentation methods. If you are *asked* to send a portfolio, do – and then make sure that you send your most professional looking materials. Consider searching online for similar materials produced by the company to see what their content looks like. You don't have to match it exactly, but if they never use GIFs, maybe you should not send a PowerPoint® deck full of them, for example.

Secondly, clean up your online presence. Do an online search for yourself and see what comes up. What social media posts did you forget to only post to friends? What comments did you make someone else's social media feed that were marked for public viewing?

Do use social media, especially LinkedIn®. Share professional posts there. Comment on your current work. Share your successes. LinkedIn® is a way to market yourself to others. If you are not using it at all, it is a signal to recruiters in the EdTech world that you are not as tech savvy as you may think. Consider posting or reacting at least once every two weeks. And, from personal experience, post from your computer, not your phone. Phone posts often result in auto-corrections that don't make any grammatical sense and appear sloppy. Use your computer and read through your posts before *and after* clicking "Post."

But never, never, *never* complain on LinkedIn®! No matter how frustrating your current position, do not post about that publicly (or even to friends, who can repost or take a screenshot.) Do not complain about recruiters or ATSs or being out of work or how you should be given a chance. You may have very valid reasons for frustration, but sharing those frustrations is not your most professional self. I have heard multiple people tell me that those who are negative online don't get an initial interview, and those who complain during the initial interview are not invited back for a second interview.

*****

TIP #11: PREPARE FOR THE INTERVIEW

With all of this preparation, what else do you need to do to prepare for the interview? Once you are invited to your first interview, there are a few tips I recommend. First and foremost, do an online search as if you were the recruiter interviewing for this position. What questions are recommended for recruiters to ask, and why? Many companies use a standard set of questions, and these questions are often the same depending on the role. I have provided a list of some of the most common questions in the appendix.

Secondly, look up the person you will be speaking with on the company's webpage and on LinkedIn®. At first, I thought this might look creepy. But then I realized that if the individual *did* notice that I had looked them up, it would show that I was preparing. I wanted to know who I was speaking with, their job title, and whether we had anything in common such as previous companies or school districts, or if we both graduated from the same university. If so, I mentioned that personal connection during my interview. (I personally don't look them up on FaceBook® or any other social media platform, though. To me, that would be crossing some professional boundaries.)

Do more research on the company. Now that you have the interview, really dig in. Is the company's history posted online? If it is a newer company, when was it founded, by whom, and why? Do you know their niche market and what market gap they are looking to address? Who are their main competitors? What is their company culture like according to sites like glassdoor.com? What do they say about themselves? How do people who work for that company speak about their experience on their own social media sites (or does everyone stay silent)? Don't forget that as you are being interviewed, you are also trying to determine if this is a good fit for you.

With most initial interviews now happening online, be sure to practice your online presence as well. Is the interview going to be held on a platform that you are less familiar with? Many online conferencing tools let you schedule a meeting for free to test it out. Ask a friend to help you. Schedule a time with a friend to run a test session using that platform. Locate the video on and off button and the mute button. (There is little that is more embarrassing than joining an online interview for an EdTech company and not knowing how to unmute yourself or turn on your camera.) Check the lighting to make sure that you have enough light *in front of you*. (If you are backlit, you will look like a witness protection program member, with your face in complete shadows. Again, not the best for an EdTech company.) And be sure to look into the camera on your device. Don't look at a second monitor or screen, and don't look at your own little video too much. Look at the camera, or just below it. It appears more natural and allows for that personal connection that is so often lacking during online sessions. (A note of caution – confirm the location of your device camera. For tablets, cameras are often on the side when you put the device in landscape mode. This can feel unnatural to look directly into the camera as you will be looking to one side or the other. I recommend using a desktop or laptop if you can, where the camera is at the top of the screen. If that is not possible, though, practice looking into the tablet camera with a friend.)

Inevitably, there will be a question about why you want to transition out of your current position. Since you do not want to be negative, how do you handle this question? There is no definite answer to give because that will differ for each of you. My advice would be to focus on what you love about teaching, what you have learned in the process that makes you desire to expand into new areas, and why their company caught your eye. Rehearse this one, literally. You want your answer to be enthusiastic about joining *their* company, not excited to leave the classroom behind, even if that is part of the reason. Look forward, not back.

Every interview ends with, "Do you have any questions for

me?" Do not say *no*. Ask a question! Show that you have been thinking and researching this company. The questions you ask will vary depending on the company and the position, but there are three questions that I asked every time I entered the interview process with a company.

First, at the initial interview I always ask what the interview process is. What can you expect next? Will there be two more interviews, or four? With whom? You may learn that at a certain stage in the interview process you will be asked to complete a mock project. Any information you can learn up front will help you prepare for the journey. If you know that they are interviewing other candidates for the next two weeks, you can relax for two weeks and not wonder why they haven't called you. If they tell you who might interview you next, you can look them up online to learn about them.

Second, I ask "the ultimate question." The ultimate question was one I learned from a friend and cheerleader of mine who supported me during my job search. She told me this question that she had learned from a friend, and it had always helped her land a job. I have to say, when I asked the question, the interviewer often responded with, "Wow! That's a great question!" So, what is the question?

In your opinion, what is the difference between a good candidate for this position and an excellent candidate for this position?

This question, and their answer, was gold to me. This caused the person interviewing me to tell me exactly what they were looking for. Sometimes their answer allowed me to understand that I would likely not be the best fit and solidified hunches that I had during the interview that I might not be happy in the position. This is valuable information for both you and the company so that you do not waste your time or theirs. But more often than not, it gave me insight into what they needed to see in me to make me that "excellent candidate." I would take notes on their response, and then – and here is the clincher – I would follow up with how delighted I was to hear that and take the opportunity to reiterate why I was an excellent candidate.

Finally, I would ask a question that made me a bit nervous but provided valuable insight. I would ask, "Is there anything that you have heard or seen today that makes you wonder if I would be an excellent candidate for this position?" I came to deeply appreciate this question because I could learn so much from their answers. Of course, I always hoped that the answer was "No, you are a perfect fit." But I *never* got that response. There was always *some* question in their minds, and that is to be expected. They are looking for an ideal candidate, and they don't know me. So, asking this question allowed me to hear their reservations and, if I could, address them. If I was lacking a skill, I would speak about how proactive I am about learning new skills and give an example of when I had done so in the past. If it was something that concerned them about a previous work experience, I had the opportunity to address how I had grown or learned from that experience. In general, I saw it as an opportunity to ask about their doubts and address them, instead of letting those doubts lead them to a rejection.

Take lots of notes during the interview. If it is the type of interview where they are sharing more information than they are asking questions, actively listen for what they need. Write down their goals for the company. Write down their goals for this position. Ask probing questions about what they are sharing with you. Engage and be interested in their mission.

After the interview, follow up! Send a thank-you email or message. Be sincere, reflecting on the conversation you had with the person. You can also take the opportunity to reiterate how you can support their mission, specifically mentioning something that stood out to you. In our virtual world, showing that you are a person who can connect with others, even if it is from behind a screen, is a valuable skill as well.

*****

TIP #12: DON'T GIVE UP

My closing advice to you is this: Don't give up! There are so many avenues for teachers to take in their own personal growth as educators. As I said at the beginning, this growth might occur by staying right in your district. Or it might occur by moving into the corporate world. Just as in education there are prime hiring seasons, so there are in the world of EdTech and educational publishing. Although jobs may become available at any time, prime hiring season for both is during the late spring and into the summer. That is when districts and companies are forecasting their needs for the upcoming school year.

If you are reading this outside of that window, don't despair. You have a tremendous opportunity ahead of you this year to build your experience. Follow the advice in these pages to prepare for a future transition. Use this time to pursue what would make you happiest. Don't worry that it hasn't happened yet. The EdTech industry is growing rapidly. Jobs and even *companies* that didn't exist yesterday will exist tomorrow and next month and next year. As you wait, keep asking questions. Keep exploring opportunities. Keep building on your skills, both digital and personal.

In the process, I truly believe you will find the next right step.

*****

REFLECTION QUESTIONS

1. Make a plan. While you are on this journey, seeking to transition into another role, what can you be doing *right now* to prepare you for and increase your chances of moving into your next role?
2. Take a look at your resume. Do you have one ready to go? If not, start writing one now. If you have one, is it "EdTech" ready? Start revising your resume before your dream job is posted.
3. What educational companies do you already know? Look at the materials you use in your classroom. Which ones do you love? Do you know who created them? Find the career pages for those companies online and bookmark them so that you can return often to see if there are openings you are interested in. (If possible, turn on notifications for job postings. You can do this on LinkedIn® and Indeed® for specific companies or job titles.)
4. Brainstorm ways you have worked with adults, especially if you have been tasked with leading a team or instructing adult learners. What additional opportunities can you take part in to build on your experience?
5. What roles do you now find yourself drawn to? Are there courses online that you can take to learn more about those roles? (Remember, these do not need to be college level courses. Signing up for some courses on LinkedIn Learning®, for example, can be incredibly valuable.)
6. Set some goals. What specific steps can you take to transition into a new field? By when will you commit to taking these steps? Break your overall goals down into smaller milestones to help you stay on track. What milestones can you set to keep moving forward?

6

APPENDIX: POSSIBLE INTERVIEW QUESTIONS

The following is a list of possible questions you might be asked in an interview for EdTech or educational publishing jobs. These questions could be asked for multiple roles. I did not provide answers for each question as you really need to make sure that your answers are not "canned." However, I did share some tips and ideas to consider.

For additional questions to help you prepare for interviews, I recommend doing an internet search for "Questions to ask during a _____ interview." Search for the questions as if you are the person doing the hiring. You will often find not only a list of questions, but also tips on what the recruiter should look for.

For all of these questions, be prepared to elaborate on your answers. Interviews are often (but not always) more of a conversation. For example, if they ask about a conflict that you have learned from, be prepared to share about that and what you have learned from the experience – but then also be prepared for follow-up questions. They might ask additional questions, like "How were you able to build on that with your team?" I cannot emphasize enough the importance of being honest during your interviews. Prepare in advance. Be real. Be professional. But most importantly, be genuinely you.

*****

THE QUESTIONS

- *What can you tell me about our product?*
  If you have had experience using the product personally in the classroom, talk about this experience and highlight what you have loved about it. If you haven't had extensive experience with the product, be sure you spend enough time learning about the product and the company itself in advance of the interview to speak to it.

- *Have you tried our product? Do you have suggestions for how we could improve it?*
  Definitely *try the product!* If you are interviewing with an EdTech company, be sure to set up a free account and then explore their product for at least 30 minutes. Create a fake class, make fake assignments, etc. Do whatever you need to do to really get a sense for how the product works and what it can offer. Take notes on your experience. What sparks joy for you? What wonderings do you have? What do you want to know more about? Don't try to fake this! Many interviewers can log into the product to see if you really have created an account and may even be able to see your activity log. No one expects you to be an expert (and trying to come off as an expert might be detrimental). However, they *do* expect that you have done some preparation to be able to speak to the product, including setting up an account. Be able to speak to how customers might benefit from the product as well as what challenges or questions they might have.

- *Tell me about a time in your career when you experienced great joy or satisfaction.*
  The recruiter is looking for a good fit. Companies want their employees to be happy because these employees generally stick around. So, the recruiter wants to see what really excites you about work to make sure that the role you are considering will really be a good fit for you. Be sure to think about this in advance and try to think of a time in your career that was deeply satisfying that would relate to the role you are applying for. As a teacher, you might feel that the most important thing to talk about is your love of teaching. You can certainly mention your love for your students, but make sure to focus on times in your career where you were working with adults in some capacity that brought you joy or satisfaction. Maybe it was when you led a curriculum planning committee. Maybe it was coaching and mentoring other teachers. Or it could even be something that you really love *outside* of the school setting that would bring value to a company, like serving on a non-profit's board of directors. If you only talk about how much you love teaching children, the recruiter will wonder why you want to now work with adults.

If your greatest satisfaction at work does not relate well to the role you are applying for, be prepared to address other aspects of your personality that might show the recruiter that this is a great fit for you. For example, maybe your greatest joy is seeing a student finally understand a difficult concept. You might not be able to relate that to applying for an entry level sales position. However, if you can also point out that you enjoy any kind of activity that involves a little bit of competition and chasing after a goal, and that you get great satisfaction out of winning a prize you've set your eye on, that might help the recruiter understand how you would be a good fit for the role.

After answering about your greatest satisfaction, be prepared to answer a follow-up question about a time in your career when you felt *least* satisfied. Answer this honestly, but don't complain about or criticize a former (or current) employer. Just explain why that particular time in your career was difficult for you, and then focus on what you learned from that experience.

- *How do you understand the role of _____?*
What many recruiters are looking for here is that you actually understand what this role does – and also that your vision aligns with the company's. Here is where you can show that you understand the nuances of the role. For example, if interviewing for customer success, speak to both the *reactive* and *proactive* nature of the customer success role as discussed in chapter 4. If you are interviewing for a content writer position, explain that you know there are two different types of content writing – educational focused and marketing focused – and if you don't already know which type of writing the position is, follow up with a question about that. For instructional design, you can speak to adult learning theory and follow up with a question about what type of model they use for their design process.

- *How would you nourish a relationship with a customer over time?*
If you will be working directly with customers (as in customer success, implementation, or sales) review the ways these roles build relationships as discussed in chapter 4. Be sure to mention having a clear understanding of the customer's goals and expectations for using the product. Then think about this the way you

would any relationship. You want to be regularly communicating, proactively reaching out, and building trust with the customer over time.

- *Tell me about an experience where you had an unhappy customer. How did you resolve their concern?*
Obviously, if you are new to EdTech or educational publishing, you may feel like you cannot answer this question. But you can! In your role as a teacher, your students *and their parents* were your customers. Can you think of a time when you had an unhappy parent? How did you resolve their concern? Recruiters are often looking for people skills here. However, they are also seeing if you are excited and motivated by challenges, or if they make you want to run away and avoid the problem.

- *If you are working with multiple customers, how would you prioritize their needs and your work?*
In many roles, you will be assigned many different accounts, whether those be schools or districts. You will need a system for tracking all your customers' needs and ensuring that you are following up with each. Even in instructional design roles, you may need to prioritize what projects to focus on to meet customer needs. Recruiters here are generally looking to see how you handle multitasking and prioritizing.

- *How might you incorporate upsells into your work?*
An "upsell" (or "soft upsell") refers to persuading customers to purchase a more expensive or premium product or to upgrade or expand the use of their product. You should always be thinking about how else the product might benefit the customer. This means that you might suggest that they expand from using a platform with a grade level or team to an entire school or district,

or that they purchase a more recent version of the product. If you work for an educational publisher, it may mean that you become familiar with the different products offered and the target audience so that you can introduce the customer to other products that would benefit them. Recruiters want to see that you can find ways to increase usage of the product(s) in ways that will truly benefit the customer.

- *Tell me about a conflict you have had with a coworker. How did you handle it?*
  Again, this question is looking for people skills and conflict-resolution skills. The ability to handle conflict well is imperative in every role.

- *What is one tech tool (or social media site) you use on a regular basis? How would you explain it to someone who is not currently using it and not tech-savvy?*
  Here is where you want to show your ability to explain a tech platform that you *do* know in a way that someone who is not familiar with it can understand.

- *Why is_____something you are interested in?*
  This is another question where the interviewer is likely looking to make sure you have a clear view of what the role is. This type of question allows you to highlight your understanding of the role in general, but also gives you the opportunity to speak to the company's direct mission and purpose and how that aligns to your passion and expertise.

- *How would you benefit our company?*
  Don't shy away from this one. The interviewer is looking to see first and foremost if you have a clear understanding of the company and its mission. Do your homework and make sure you can clearly state what the

company's mission and vision are. Speak to its niche market. Be prepared (by researching ahead of time) to speak to any recent challenges or changes that you might be able to support. For example, did the company recently create a new curriculum for preschool students? This would be a great opportunity to share that you are certified and experienced with Pre-K.

- *How many first graders in the United States eat pickles? (Or any odd question about numbers or estimates)*
  I have never been asked this question, but others have warned me about it. This question is not a trick question! There is no definite right answer. Don't be thrown off. Instead, know that what the interviewer is looking for is your ability to think on your feet and take action even when you have limited information to try to solve a problem. You can ask follow-up questions, but then show your thinking as you create a best guess at your answer. It doesn't really matter if you get the correct answer. What matters is that you show your thought process.

  So, for example, you might ask if they mean just dill pickles or all pickles. Then work through your thinking aloud. "I can estimate that there are about 300 million people in the United States, all between the ages of 0-100. If 1% of that population is between 6-7, that would be a total of about 3,000,000 first graders in the United States. Now, based on experience, I would say that most, but not all kids, like eating pickles. I am going to estimate that about 80 percent of kids eat pickles based on experience. So, that would be somewhere around 2.5 million first graders."

- *Give an example of when you served in a leadership role and had to make a decision, solve a problem, etc.*

This is where you want to highlight any leadership roles you have had in the past. Be prepared for this question! Think about a difficult decision that you had to make in leadership or a challenge you had to overcome and prepare in advance to share about it. Consulting involves working with a team, identifying challenges and obstacles, and finding solutions to these problems. How have you done that in your role as an educator? If you don't have experience in an administrative position, have you served as a team leader or been a committee member tasked with training your colleagues? Don't focus on your students during this question. You want to be able to show that you can lead adults.

- *Give an example of a professional mistake you have made, and how have you grown from it?*
  Try to be specific without going into too much detail. Focus on the lesson you learned so that you can show that you embrace opportunities for growth.

- *Why do you want to work for this company? (What attracted you to our company?)*
  This question is not about the position. It's about what you know about the company's mission and culture – and how you see yourself fitting into that culture.

- *What would you do if you were presenting to a group of teachers and one or two of them were obviously frustrated?*
  This question is looking to see how you might handle pushback from some of your adult learners. Do you have the skills to diffuse a difficult situation and the confidence to keep going while also empathizing with those who are expressing frustration? Do you seek to understand their needs, but also have the ability to keep moving forward?

- *Based on your knowledge of the EdTech/educational publishing sector, who are our biggest competitors?*
  I cannot stress this enough – research the company before you interview. Make sure you know enough about them to answer this question. If you have experience with a competitor's product, speak to that experience and add why you think this company has more to offer their customers.

- *What interests you in the EdTech sector?*
  You want to be able to show that interviewing for this position is not just an exit strategy from a difficult situation. Have you been following EdTech companies for years? Have you attended EdTech conferences? Have you been excited by using products in your classroom and seeing the impact they have on students? Show your passion and excitement here.

- *What questions do you have for me?*
  Make sure to ask questions! I've shared many different ideas in this book for specific roles. Ask about what the day in the life of someone in this role might look like and why your interviewer enjoys working for this company. Also ask the question about the difference between a good candidate and an exceptional candidate.

- *What is your salary requirement for this position?*
  This is a tricky question and can be awkward to answer. Research before the interview what the salary range for this position is in your area and consider looking at salary reporting sites like Glassdoor® that often share information from company employees on their salaries. Keep in mind that you are new to the field. Instead of providing a specific number, give the interviewer a salary range that you are willing to consider.

If you need to ask *them* about the salary, ask "What is the allocated salary range for this position?" Hiring managers often need to get budget approval for a new position, so there is usually an allocated range. In entry-level positions, there is often not a whole lot of wiggle room.

ENDNOTES

[1] Frustration in the Schools: Teachers Speak Out on Pay, Funding and Feeling Valued (Arlington, Virginia: PDK International, 2019), https://pdkpoll.org/.

[2] "School Workforce in England," Explore Education Statistics, https://explore-education-statistics.service.gov.uk/find-statistics/school-workforce-in-england.

[3] Montgomery McCarthy and Larry Akinyooye, "Job Openings, Hires, and Quits Set Record Highs in 2019," Monthly Labor Review, U.S. Bureau of Labor Statistics, June 2020, https://doi.org/10.21916/mlr.2020.12.

[4] Abigail Johnson Hess, "Workers Quit Their Jobs at the Fastest Rate on Record in 2019—Here's Why," Make It, January 8, 2020, https://www.cnbc.com/2020/01/07/workers-quit-their-jobs-at-the-fastest-rate-on-record-in-2019.html.

[5] Liana Loewus, "Participation in Teachers' Unions Is Down, and Likely to Tumble Further," Education Week, October 12, 2017, https://www.edweek.org/leadership/participation-in-teachers-unions-is-down-and-likely-to-tumble-further/2017/10.

[6] "Professional, Scientific and Technical Services: NAICS 54," U.S. Bureau of Labor Statistics, https://www.bls.gov/iag/tgs/iag54.htm.

[7] "Digest of Education Statistics: 2019," National Center for Education Statistics, Table 211.60, https://nces.ed.gov/programs/digest/d19/tables/dt19_211.60.asp.

[8] "What Is the Average Customer Success Manager Salary by State," ZipRecruiter, https://www.ziprecruiter.com/Salaries/What-Is-the-Average-Customer-Success-Manager-Salary-by-State.

[9] "What Is the Average Customer Success Manager Salary by State," ZipRecruiter.

[10] "When Elementary and Secondary Students Go Back to School," Pew Research Center, August 14, 2019, https://www.pewresearch.org/fact-tank/2019/08/14/back-to-school-dates-u-s/ft_19-08-09_schoolstartdates_1_2/.

[11] "2019 Most Stressful Jobs," CareerCast, https://www.careercast.com/jobs-rated/most-stressful-jobs-2019.

[12] "Jobs Rated Methodology," CareerCast, https://www.careercast.com/jobs-rated/most-stressful-jobs-2019.

[13] "High School Teachers," Occupational Outlook Handbook, U.S. Bureau of Labor Statistics, https://www.bls.gov/ooh/education-training-and-library/high-school-teachers.htm; "Kindergarten and Elementary School Teachers," Occupational Outlook Handbook, U.S.

Bureau of Labor Statistics, https://www.bls.gov/ooh/education-training-and-library/kindergarten-and-elementary-school-teachers.htm.

[14] "Elementary, Middle, and High School Principals," Occupational Outlook Handbook, U.S. Bureau of Labor Statistics, https://www.bls.gov/ooh/management/elementary-middle-and-high-school-principals.htm.

[15] "School and Career Counselors and Advisors," Occupational Outlook Handbook, U.S. Bureau of Labor Statistics, https://www.bls.gov/ooh/community-and-social-service/school-and-career-counselors.htm.

[16] Kency Nittler, "How Do School Districts Compensate Teachers for Advanced Degrees?" National Council on Teacher Quality, July 26, 2018, https://www.nctq.org/blog/How-do-school-districts-compensate-teachers-for-advanced-degrees.

[17] "Instructional Coach Salary," ZipRecruiter, https://www.ziprecruiter.com/Salaries/Instructional-Coach-Salary.

[18] "K-12 Curriculum Developer: Job Description and Salary Information," Resilient Educator, September 1, 2020, https://resilienteducator.com/teaching-careers/k-12-curriculum-developer/.

[19] "Instructional Coordinators," Occupational Outlook Handbook, U.S. Bureau of Labor Statistics, https://www.bls.gov/ooh/education-training-and-library/instructional-coordinators.htm.

[20] Angela Chen, "The Ever-Growing Ed-Tech Market," The Atlantic, November 6, 2015, https://www.theatlantic.com/education/archive/2015/11/quantifying-classroom-tech-market/414244/.

[21] "Education Technology Market Size, Share & Trends Analysis Report by Sector (Preschool, K-12, Higher Education), by End User (Business, Consumer), by Type (Hardware, Software), by Region, and Segment Forecasts, 2021 – 2028," Grand View Research, April 2021, https://www.grandviewresearch.com/industry-analysis/education-technology-market.

[22] Education Technology Use in Schools: Student and Educator Perspectives (Washington, DC: Gallup, 2019), https://www.newschools.org/wp-content/uploads/2020/03/Gallup-Ed-Tech-Use-in-Schools-2.pdf.

[23] "The EdTech Report," RS Components, https://uk.rs-online.com/web/generalDisplay.html?id=did-you-know/the-edtech-report.

[24] Hotels4Teams, https://www.hotels4teams.com/editorschoice/too-many-hotel-brands/; Alex Kopestinsky, "The State of Insurance

Industry – 2021 (Statistics and Facts)," PolicyAdvice, August 8, 2021, https://policyadvice.net/insurance/insights/insurance-industry/.

[25] "Education Publishers' Directory," PublishersGlobal, https://www.publishersglobal.com/directory/subject/education-publishers.

[26] "The Definition of Customer Success," Customer Success Association, https://www.customersuccessassociation.com/library/the-definition-of-customer-success/.

[27] "The History of Customer Success – Part I," Customer Success Association, https://www.customersuccessassociation.com/library/the-history-of-customer-success-part-1/.

[28] "Customer Success Manager," Salary.com, https://www.salary.com/tools/salary-calculator/customer-success-manager.

[29] "What Is the Average Customer Success Manager Salary by State," ZipRecruiter, https://www.ziprecruiter.com/Salaries/What-Is-the-Average-Customer-Success-Manager-Salary-by-State.

[30] "Implementation Specialist Salaries," Glassdoor, https://www.glassdoor.com/Salaries/implementation-specialist-salary-SRCH_KO0,25.htm; "How Much Does an Implementation Specialist Make in the United States?" Indeed, https://www.indeed.com/career/implementation-specialist/salaries; "Implementation Specialist I," Salary.com, https://www.salary.com/research/salary/benchmark/implementation-specialist-i-salary.

[31] "Professional Services Consultant I," Salary.com, https://www.salary.com/tools/salary-calculator/professional-services-consultant-i.

[32] "Consultant Salary," ZipRecruiter, https://www.ziprecruiter.com/Salaries/Consultant-Salary.

[33] "Writers and Authors," Occupational Outlook Handbook, U.S. Bureau of Labor Statistics, https://www.bls.gov/ooh/media-and-communication/writers-and-authors.htm.

[34] "How Do You Become an Instructional Designer?" Khan Academy, https://www.khanacademy.org/college-careers-more/career-content/educate/career-profile-instructional-designer/a/how-do-you-become-an-instructional-designer.

[35] Marina Arshavskiy, "Measuring eLearning Effectiveness: How Key Performance Indicators (KPIs) Can Help Validate Investment Decisions," eLearning Industry, https://elearningindustry.com/measuring-elearning-key-performance-indicators.

[36] "How Much Does an Instructional Designer Make in the United States?" Indeed, https://www.indeed.com/career/instructional-designer/salaries; "How Much Does a Instructional Designer Make?" Glassdoor, https://www.glassdoor.com/Salaries/instructional-designer-salary-SRCH_KO0,22.htm.

[37] "How Remote Workers Are Paid: Location-Based and Job-Based Pay," Glassdoor, July 15, 2021, https://www.glassdoor.com/blog/paid-location-and-job-based-pay-for-remote-workers/.

[38] "Training and Development Specialists," Occupational Outlook Handbook, U.S. Bureau of Labor Statistics, https://www.bls.gov/ooh/business-and-financial/training-and-development-specialists.htm.

[39] "Training and Development Managers," Occupational Outlook Handbook, U.S. Bureau of Labor Statistics, https://www.bls.gov/ooh/management/training-and-development-managers.htm.

[40] Jake Bryant and Judy Wade, "The High Performing Ed Tech Sales Rep," Fuel, April 10, 2017, https://get.fuelbymckinsey.com/article/the-high-performing-ed-tech-sales-rep-it-isnt-who-you-think-it-is/.

[41] Bryant and Wade, "High Performing Ed Tech Sales Rep."

[42] "How Much Does a Educational Sales Make?" Glassdoor, https://www.glassdoor.com/Salaries/educational-sales-salary-SRCH_KO0,17.htm.

[43] "The Education & Technology Sales Compensation and Industry Status Report 2020," Renaissance Network, https://ren-network.com/education-technology-sales-compensation-2020/.

[44] Somen Mondal, "The 25 Top Recruiting Software Tools of 2021," Ideal, January 14, 2021, https://ideal.com/top-recruiting-software/.

[45] Mondal, "25 Top Recruiting Software Tools of 2021."

Made in the USA
Las Vegas, NV
11 December 2023

82597224R00075